Overcoming Your Alcohol or Drug Problem

Effective Recovery Strategies   SECOND EDITION

Workbook

Dennis C. Daley • G. Alan Marlatt

UNIVERSITY PRESS

2006

OXFORD
UNIVERSITY PRESS

Oxford University Press, Inc., publishes works that further
Oxford University's objective of excellence
in research, scholarship, and education.

Oxford   New York
Auckland   Cape Town   Dar es Salaam   Hong Kong   Karachi
Kuala Lumpur   Madrid   Melbourne   Mexico City   Nairobi
New Delhi   Shanghai   Taipei   Toronto

With offices in
Argentina   Austria   Brazil   Chile   Czech Republic   France   Greece
Guatemala   Hungary   Italy   Japan   Poland   Portugal   Singapore
South Korea   Switzerland   Thailand   Turkey   Ukraine   Vietnam

Copyright © 2006 by Oxford University Press, Inc.

Published by Oxford University Press, Inc.
198 Madison Avenue, New York, New York 10016

www.oup.com

Oxford is a registered trademark of Oxford University Press

ISBN 978–0–19–530774–0

9 8 7 6 5 4

Printed in the United States of America
on acid-free paper

Overcoming Your Alcohol or Drug Problem

About Treatments *ThatWork*™

One of the most difficult problems confronting patients with various disorders and diseases is finding the best help available. Everyone is aware of friends or family who have sought treatment from a seemingly reputable practitioner, only to find out later from another doctor that the original diagnosis was wrong or the treatments recommended were inappropriate or perhaps even harmful. Most patients, or family members, address this problem by reading everything they can about their symptoms, seeking out information on the Internet, or aggressively "asking around" to tap knowledge from friends and acquaintances. Governments and healthcare policymakers are also aware that people in need don't always get the best treatments, something they refer to as "variability in healthcare practices."

Now healthcare systems around the world are attempting to correct this variability by introducing "evidence-based practice." This simply means that it is in everyone's interest that patients get the most up-to-date and effective care for a particular problem. Healthcare policymakers have also recognized that it is very useful to give consumers of healthcare as much information as possible, so that they can make intelligent decisions in a collaborative effort to improve health and mental health. This series, "Treatments *ThatWork*™," is designed to accomplish just that. Only the latest and most effective interventions for particular problems are described in user-friendly language. To be included in this series, each treatment program must pass the highest standards of evidence available, as determined by a scientific advisory board. Thus, when individuals suffering from these problems or their family members seek out an expert clinician who is familiar with these interventions and decides that they are appropriate, they will have confidence that they are receiving the best care available. Of course, only your healthcare professional can decide on the right mix of treatments for you.

The ravages of alcohol, tobacco, and drug abuse have been documented time and again, and the lives ruined are too numerous to count. But new treatment programs have appeared in the last decade that have been proven to be effective in relieving the burden of abuse and addiction for a large number of individuals. The program described in this manual presents the latest version of one of the most advanced treatment programs yet developed for problems with alcohol, tobacco, or drugs. This program recognizes that these problems have both biological and psychological causes, and that no single program will work the same for everyone. Therefore it is meant to be flexibly adapted to where the individual is on the long road to recovery, from just getting started through preventing relapse. Incorporating the wisdom of programs that have come before such as 12-step programs, cognitive–behavioral programs, and relapse prevention approaches, this treatment benefits from decades of development and scientific evaluation and has been used to the benefit of thousands of individuals with these problems. In this program you will learn skills to cope effectively with cues and triggers that lead to use and abuse of drugs and alcohol and hopefully master the emotional roller coaster that accompanies this condition. This includes altering patterns of beliefs, dealing with interpersonal conflicts that often lead to use and abuse, and building healthy social support systems. This program is most effectively applied by working in collaboration with your clinician.

David H. Barlow, Editor-in-Chief,
Treatments *ThatWork*™
Boston, Massachusetts

Acknowledgments

We wish to thank Judith Gordon, Ph.D., and Natalie Daley, M.S.W., for their helpful critiques of the first edition of this workbook. We also wish to thank David Barlow, Ph.D., for his interest in this project. Finally we wish to acknowledge Mariclaire Cloutier, Cristina Wojdylo, and Rosanne Hallowell of Oxford University Press.

Contents

Overview of Substance Use Problems and Assessment

Chapter 1   *Introduction and Plan for Workbook*

Goals

- To understand the characteristics of substance use problems

- To understand the benefits of using this workbook in conjunction with supervised therapy or counseling

- To learn the importance of keeping records and completing recovery worksheets

Introduction and Overview

This recovery workbook provides you with practical information and skills to help you understand and change your problem with alcohol, tobacco, or other drugs such as marijuana, cocaine, pills, or heroin. It is designed to be used in therapy or counseling and will help you focus on specific issues involved in stopping substance use and in changing behaviors or aspects of your lifestyle that keep your substance use problem active. The information presented in this workbook is derived from research studies of substance abuse treatment and our many years of experience working with clients who have alcohol, tobacco, and other drug problems. It discusses the most effective and helpful recovery issues and change strategies from studies of cognitive–behavioral treatment, coping skills training, 12-step counseling, and relapse prevention. These studies focus on the importance of changing beliefs, thinking, relationships, and behaviors and learning "skills" to help you stay sober and change your life.

Your change plan should be tailored to your needs and problems. No single recovery program is for everyone. The ideas in this workbook will help you work with a therapist or counselor to develop your personal plan for recovery.

In this workbook, we provide you with information about substance use problems, the recovery process, the relapse process, types of professional treatments available, and self-help groups. When we talk about "substance use problems," we are referring to problems with alcohol, tobacco, or any other type of drug. Although there are differences among the various substance use problems, there are also many similarities. Therefore, the recovery strategies discussed throughout this workbook can be adapted to any type of substance-related problem. The major goals of this workbook are to help you reach maximum treatment benefit by motivating you to develop and implement a personal change plan and to provide you with practical strategies or skills to cope with the most common problems and challenges encountered when substance use is stopped.

This workbook includes the following topics:

- Recognizing your substance use problem and the consequences of it

- Choosing the right treatment setting

- Managing your cravings

- Controlling thoughts of using alcohol or drugs

- Dealing with upsetting emotions (anger, boredom, depression, etc.)

- Refusing offers to use substances

- Dealing with family and interpersonal conflicts

- Building a recovery support system

- Identifying and managing relapse warning signs and high-risk factors

- Relapse management

- Living a balanced life

- Measuring your progress

- Managing a co-existing psychiatric disorder

Definition and Prevalence of Substance Use Problems

A substance use problem exists when you experience any type of difficulty related to using alcohol, tobacco, or other drugs, including illicit street drugs or prescribed drugs such as painkillers or tranquilizers. The difficulty can be in any area of your life: medical or physical, psychological, family, interpersonal, social, academic, occupational, legal, financial, or spiritual.

Substance abuse and substance dependence are clinical diagnoses used when your problematic use of substances meets specific criteria in the *Diagnostic and Statistical Manual of Mental Disorder, Fourth Edition, Text Revision (DSM-IV-TR)*.

Substance abuse is diagnosed when your pattern of use leads to significant impairment or distress, evidenced by meeting one or more of the following criteria within a 12-month period of time:

- Your recurrent use of alcohol or other drugs leads to failure to fulfill your major obligations at work, school, or home.

- You drink or take drugs in situations in which it is physically hazardous to do so.

- Your use causes legal problems.

- You continue to drink alcohol or take drugs even though they are causing social or relationship problems in your life.

Substance dependence is diagnosed when you meet three or more of the following criteria:

- Your tolerance to alcohol or drugs increases (takes you more to get high or achieve the desired effect of using alcohol or other substances).

- Your tolerance to alcohol or drugs decreases (you are affected by smaller quantities than in the past).

- You suffer withdrawal symptoms when you cut down or stop using alcohol or drugs.

- You keep using substances to avoid withdrawal sickness.

- You lose control over how much you use or for what length of time you use.

- You have difficulty cutting down or controlling your substance use.

- You are preoccupied with using or getting substances.

- You experience social, work, or recreational problems as a result of your use.

- You continue to use despite negative effects of such use.

The main difference between abuse and dependence is that the latter involves more symptoms and negative effects than abuse and often involves physiological symptoms such as tolerance change or withdrawal symptoms. Examples of each of the symptoms of abuse and dependence are provided in the next chapter along with a checklist so that you can note which symptoms you are currently experiencing.

Although many types of substances can be abused and can cause physical or psychological dependence, the most commonly abused substances are alcohol, tobacco, marijuana, and cocaine. Almost 14% of adults in our country will experience an alcohol abuse or dependency problem, and over 6% will experience a drug abuse or dependency problem. The majority of smokers in the United States are considered dependent. Many people have problems with two or more substances.

Causes of Substance Use Problems

There is no single cause of all alcohol or drug problems. These problems are caused by a number of different biological, psychological, and social or environmental factors that vary from one person to the next.

Biological Causes

Alcohol problems run in families, so it is thought that some individuals have a genetic predisposition to develop an alcohol problem. Keep in mind that no one specific "alcohol" or "drug dependence" gene has yet been identified. However, it is likely that there are differences in brain chemistry and metabolism that increase the likelihood of developing an addiction to alcohol or other substances. Scientists believe that these addictive substances work on the mesolimbic dopamine pathway or "reward" pathway of the brain. This is the part of the brain that makes food, sex, and social activities pleasurable. As addiction progresses, the brain is "hijacked" by substances. The result is that the addicted person relies more on substances and less on natural rewards to feel good. Even though substance use causes many problems, it is then "reinforced" when the person ingests alcohol or drugs. Some addicted people also develop a tolerance for alcohol or other drugs, requiring an increasing amount of alcohol or drugs to obtain the desired effect. Their bodies seem to "need" or "want" substances, unlike people who do not develop an addiction or dependency on substances.

Psychological Causes

Substances are often used to reduce anxiety or tension, to relax, to cope with other unpleasant feelings, or to escape. For some people, this eventually contributes to substance abuse or dependency as they get more accustomed to using alcohol, tobacco, or other drugs to feel normal. Others have certain personality traits that make them more prone to using and subsequently abusing substances. Some have a psychiatric disorder, which can increase their vulnerability to developing a substance disorder.

Social or Environmental Causes

The family and social environment in which we live influences most behaviors, including substance use behavior. A person's decision to use or not to use substances is affected by access to substances, pressure from peers to use, reinforcement from peers for using, observance of role models (e.g., parents) abusing substances, and standards or values learned from the community or broader culture.

Multiple Causes

Most likely it is not one but a combination of factors that caused you to develop a substance use problem. In cases of addiction or dependency, the factors that contributed to your initial use may be totally different than those that cause you to continue using. For some people physical factors may be the strongest, whereas for others psychological or social factors may be the strongest. Identifying the factors that contribute to your substance use problem can contribute to your recovery.

Benefits of This Workbook

This workbook offers many benefits, especially when used with professional therapy or counseling. First, it will help you become more educated about substance use problems and recovery. Understanding the recovery process, for example, makes it easier to cope with the ups and downs you are likely to experience. Second, this workbook will help you take a look at your particular problem with alcohol, tobacco, or other drugs and identify how it has affected your life and the lives of people close to you. Third, it will help you learn specific skills to manage the challenges and "nuts and bolts" problems encountered in recovery. Finally, it will help you reduce the risk of a future relapse. As a result of working a recovery program, you can experience benefits in your physical, emotional, or spiritual health; family and social relationships; ability to work or go to school; and financial condition. There are many potential short-term and long-term benefits of recovery.

Tips on Using This Workbook in Your Treatment

Overcoming Your Alcohol or Drug Problem: Effective Recovery Strategies, Workbook, Second Edition, was written to be used in conjunction with therapy or counseling. Ask your therapist or counselor for help in choosing which topics to work on and in what sequence. The sequence you choose should be based on your unique problems with substance use and where you are in the recovery process. If you have any questions about the meaning of the information presented, how it relates to your situation, or how to use it to aid your recovery, ask your therapist. If you try to implement some of the change strategies recommended and find they aren't working for you, work with your therapist to figure out why these ideas aren't helpful or if you need to find other strategies. Even if you don't agree with what you read in this workbook, you will find it helpful to discuss your reactions and ideas with your therapist.

This workbook can be used whether you are in individual or group therapy, or both. An open, honest, realistic, and disciplined approach to recovery in which you face your issues rather than avoid them will help you make the most progress.

Abstinence from the use of substances is usually the most appropriate goal of treatment, especially if you have an addiction. However, some people initially benefit from a harm-reduction approach before they agree on abstinence. Harm reduction refers to a reduction in the amount and frequency of substance use so there is a reduction in the negative consequences such as medical, family, work, or legal problems. However, if you are addicted, there is always the risk that serious consequences or even death could result if you do not stop completely.

The Importance of Keeping Records and Completing Recovery Worksheets

Throughout this recovery workbook, you will be asked to complete a number of records and worksheets related to each area of recovery. These assignments have several purposes:

1. To help you personalize the information presented so that you relate it to your unique situation. The information presented will make the most sense if you can relate it to your individual circumstances.

2. To help you become aware of the many aspects of recovery and of the relationship between thoughts, feelings, and behaviors. We use the biopsychosocial model, in which biological, psychological, social, and spiritual aspects of recovery are all emphasized as important to your well-being and continued progress.

3. To help you identify internal and external triggers of substance use and develop strategies to manage them.

4. To provide you with a reminder that you need to take an active role in stopping alcohol and drug use and learn to cope positively with the problems experienced in recovery.

5. To help you carry out the proposed recovery change techniques and practice them in your daily life.

6. To help you document problems as well as successes with specific changes. Keeping track of your progress over time allows you to see the "big picture" and put setbacks into perspective.

7. To help you approach your treatment in a systematic and structured way. This allows you to take maximum advantage of your therapy

sessions because you are always working on important recovery issues between treatment sessions.

This interactive recovery workbook can be used as your personal notebook to keep track of important issues in your quest to manage your substance use problem. You can revisit sections of this workbook as many times as you need to help yourself develop and modify your change plan. When you are finished with professional treatment, this workbook can serve as a reminder for you. After a period of time, you can go back, review, and add to it as you learn new ways to handle the problems and demands of recovery.

Chapter 2   *Recognizing Your Substance Use Problem*

Goals

▨ To understand the different categories and symptoms of substance use disorders

▨ To rate the overall severity of your substance use problem

Continuum of Substance Use Problems

The American Psychiatric Association classifies substance use disorders into several different categories. These include the following:

▨ Intoxication

▨ Withdrawal

▨ Substance abuse

▨ Substance dependence

▨ Substance-induced mood, anxiety, and psychotic disorders, and personality disorders

As you will see in the sections that follow, each category has its own set of symptoms. Substance use problems can be classified from mild or moderate to severe or life-threatening. After you have read this chapter, complete the Self-Rating Scale.

Intoxication and Withdrawal

Intoxication refers to being "drunk," "stoned," "loaded," or "under the influence" of alcohol or other drugs. It involves physiological signs such as slurred speech and incoordination with alcohol or other sedatives or hypnotics; elevated blood pressure with cocaine or other stimulants; or drowsiness or slurred speech with opiates. Intoxication also involves psychological or behavioral changes such as aggressiveness, irritability, impaired attention, or disturbance of mood. Intoxication affects judgment and in some cases can contribute to the occurrence of serious behaviors such as violence toward others, accidents, or suicide attempts.

Withdrawal symptoms are caused by stopping or reducing the intake of substances that produce physical dependence (e.g., alcohol, heroin). Specific withdrawal symptoms are discussed in Chapter 15 (which also addresses medications used in the treatment of substance use problems).

Symptoms of Substance Abuse

If your pattern of substance use leads to significant impairment in your life or to personal distress but does not meet the criteria for dependence (see criteria for substance dependence in the next section), you meet the criteria for a substance abuse problem. Often, but not always, a pattern of abuse will worsen and turn into a dependency problem over time. Substance abuse is diagnosed if one or more of the four criteria listed on p. 13 occur within a 12-month period. As you read these criteria, note whether or not you have experienced each of them by placing a check mark in the appropriate box.

Case Examples

Randy (Alcohol Abuse)

Randy is a 41-year-old, married father of two with a 16-year history of alcohol use. He owns a small home improvement business and employs four other men. Randy first drank at age 15 and first became intoxicated at age 17. He drank moderately until his early 30s, at which time he increased the frequency and amount of alcohol intake from several drinks per month to regular weekend use of six or more beers, and occasional weekday use of four or more beers per drinking occasion. During the past year and a half, Randy has had several weekend binges leading to bad hangovers, causing him to miss work and pay less attention to his business than usual. He and his wife began arguing over his alcohol use and his failure to spend time with her and the

Substance Abuse Criteria

Criterion 1: Failure to Fulfill Major Obligations ☐ Yes ☒ No

You do not fulfill your obligations at work, home, or school. Examples include repeated absences or poor performance at school or work, suspensions or expulsions from school, and neglect of your children or household responsibilities.

Criterion 2: Use in Hazardous Situations ☒ Yes ☐ No

You use substances in physically hazardous situations. Examples include driving a vehicle or operating a machine when impaired by substance use.

Criterion 3: Legal Problems ☐ Yes ☒ No

You have recurrent substance-related legal problems. Examples include arrests for disorderly conduct and driving under the influence of alcohol or drugs.

Criterion 4: Continued Use Despite Problems ☐ Yes ☒ No

You have recurrent social or interpersonal problems that are caused by or worsened by substance use. Examples include marital conflicts and physical fights.

Write the number of symptoms for which you checked "Yes". _____1_____

children on weekends. Often on weekends, after going to potential customers' homes to give estimates, Randy stops at local bars and clubs and drinks with his friends. ▓

Jenny (Marijuana Abuse)

▓ *Jenny is a 17-year-old high school senior who uses marijuana several times per month. During the past several months her use has increased, and she often drinks alcohol along with smoking marijuana to get a better high. Jenny has driven while high on marijuana, and her interest in partying has led to a decrease in her grades and arguments with her parents. Jenny has a sexually transmitted disease as a result of getting drunk and having un-protected sex with boys she met at parties.* ▓

Substance Dependence

DSM-IV-TR gives seven criteria for substance dependence. The symptoms described are part of a problematic pattern of substance use that leads to

Substance Dependence Criteria

Criterion 1(a): Increased Tolerance   ☒ Yes   ☐ No

ATIVAN

You need more of the substance to achieve the desired effect. Examples:

1. John used to get high on two or three drinks. He now often consumes six or more drinks before he feels high.
2. Wanda used to take two tablets of Valium per day. She now takes six and often uses other tranquilizers and alcohol, because two pills don't do anything for her.

Criterion 1(b): Decreased Effect   ☐ Yes   ☒ No

You experience a diminished effect with continued use of the same amount of a substance. Examples:

1. Delinda used to drink a pint or more of liquor every day to feel "the buzz." Now, when she drinks the same amount, she does not feel "the buzz" as before.
2. Alphonso regularly used large quantities of opiate drugs, alcohol, and tranquilizers in the past. Now when he uses the same quantities, he does not even feel high.

Criterion 2(a): Withdrawal Sickness   ☒ Yes   ☐ No

You experience a specific withdrawal symptom when you stop using or cut down on the amount you use. Examples:

1. When Michelle stops using alcohol, she becomes nauseous and anxious and has tremors.
2. Russ gets stomach cramps, diarrhea, a runny nose, and gooseflesh when he stops injecting heroin or other narcotic drugs.

Criterion 2(b): Use to Avoid Withdrawal Sickness   ☒ Yes   ☐ No

You continuously use a substance, use similar types of chemicals (e.g., you substitute Valium for alcohol), or use first thing in the morning to avoid being sick with withdrawal symptoms. Examples:

1. Betty takes tranquilizers constantly because she's afraid she will get sick if she doesn't always have them in her system.
2. Dean takes a few belts of whiskey in his coffee every morning to quell his shakes and get him settled down so he can go to work. At lunch he has a few drinks to hold him over until after work when he can drink more freely.

Criterion 3: Loss of Control   ☐ Yes   ☒ No

You use a greater quantity of alcohol or drugs than you intended or for longer periods of time than you intended. Examples:

1. Ron bought an ounce of marijuana and planned to use it over a period of several months but ended up smoking it all in less than a week.
2. Lisa constantly tells herself she's going to have only a few drinks at parties each weekend, but she always gets drunk.

Criterion 4: Inability to Cut Down or Control Use   ☒ Yes   ☐ No

You try to cut down but succeed for only short periods of time. You quit, only to go back to using again. Examples:

1. Dennis has quit smoking at least 10 times in the past few years for periods from several days to 3 months, but he always goes back to smoking.

2. Liz buys a $10 rock of crack cocaine when she gets her check with the intention of not smoking more than that amount. However, she always ends up purchasing more crack and more often than not uses her entire check to buy the drug, smoking continuously until she runs out of drugs and money.

Criterion 5: Preoccupation or Compulsion ☒ Yes ☒ No

You spend a great deal of time on activities necessary to obtain the substance, use the substance, or recover from its effects. Examples:

1. Sandy, a nurse in a large hospital, spends a considerable amount of time figuring out ways to steal narcotic drugs at work to support her habit.
2. Stephen plans his work day so that he's able to use cocaine at several points. Also, his weekends are almost entirely dedicated to getting high on drugs.

Criterion 6: Psychosocial Impairment ☐ Yes ☒ No

You give up or lose important social, occupational, or recreational activities because of substance use. Examples:

1. Melissa has lost two jobs due to absenteeism caused by alcohol use. She has also quit swimming and playing tennis.
2. Leonard, once a star athlete with a promising college career, was kicked off the football team because he tested positive for drugs on three different occasions. As a result, he also lost his scholarship and dropped out of college.

Criterion 7: Continued Use Despite Negative Effects ☒ Yes ☐ No

You continue to use even though you know that a physical, psychological, family, or other problem is likely to occur as a result. Examples:

1. Don continues to drink despite warnings from his physician that his liver was damaged from years of excessive drinking.
2. Roberta continues to smoke over two packs of cigarettes each day despite recommendations from her physician to stop because of chronic respiratory problems.

Write the number of symptoms that you checked "Yes" for. 4 - 5 _____

significant impairment or personal distress. Three or more of the seven criteria must occur within a 12-month period for substance dependence to be diagnosed. As you read these criteria and the examples, note whether or not you have experienced each of them by placing a check mark in the appropriate box.

Remember, you can meet criteria for dependence without having a physical addiction. If you meet three or more of the above criteria within a 12-month period, you have substance dependency. Dependence should not be seen as something you either have or do not have. In reality, there are many degrees to which you can be dependent on substances. Like medical problems such as diabetes, asthma, or cancer or psychiatric problems such as depression or anxiety, the severity of substance dependence can range from mild to extremely severe. The Self-Rating Scale at the end of this chapter can help you rate the overall severity of your substance use problem. Also, the case examples in this and the following chapter clearly illustrate how the effects of substance use can vary from one person to the next, from mild to life-threatening.

Case Examples

Nicole (Tobacco and Alcohol Dependence)

Nicole is a 55-year-old, divorced mother of two adult children and grandmother of five. She had a history of over 30 years of alcohol dependence. Nicole drank on a daily basis, consuming up to a case of beer at a time during her worst period of drinking. Her tolerance was quite high for many years, although in the final years of drinking her tolerance actually decreased. She also experienced withdrawal tremors and would often drink in the morning to stop them. Her alcohol use contributed to severe family conflict, an inability to function as an effective mother when her children were young, financial problems, depression, suicidal feelings, and an inability to hold a job. Nicole has been sober for over 1 year and her life has improved modestly. She now wants to address her dependence on nicotine. She has been smoking two to three packs of cigarettes a day for "too many years to count." Nicole reports her dependence on nicotine has caused her to have problems with shortness of breath when she walks long distances or up stairs; has made her more susceptible to a variety of minor physical ailments; has been a factor in heated arguments with one of her adult sons, who refuses to bring his children to visit her "smoke-filled house"; and is using up too much of her limited income.

Steve (Opiate Dependence and Polydrug Abuse)

Steve is a 36-year-old, divorced physician who began using alcohol and marijuana during high school. His use increased during college and medical school, but he managed to make excellent grades, mainly due to his intellectual ability. During the latter part of his medical internship, Steve began snorting heroin and cocaine occasionally. This pattern continued fairly steadily when he joined a medical practice. During the past several years, Steve used Percocet on a daily basis. He also began shooting heroin intravenously and couldn't function without opiates in his system. Steve used a variety of other drugs to reduce his anxiety, insomnia, and stress. However, drugs eventually became the central organizing factor in his life. Prior to entering treatment involuntarily, his drug dependence cost him his marriage. To continue practicing medicine, he is required by a state regulatory agency to maintain abstinence from all illicit drugs and alcohol, participate in treatment, and submit regular urine samples to verify his abstinence. ▨

Substance-Induced Mood, Anxiety, and Psychotic Disorders, and Personality Disorders

The effects of alcohol and other drugs on the central nervous system can cause substance-induced mood, anxiety, and psychotic disorders, or magnify personality disorders. What this essentially means is that symptoms that look like a psychiatric illness develop but clear up with continued abstinence from alcohol or other drugs. This is why several weeks or longer is often needed to help determine if a depression or anxiety syndrome is an independent psychiatric disorder or is caused by the chronic use of substances. For example, Matt felt extremely depressed and suicidal following several weeks of using cocaine on a daily basis. However, within a week of stopping cocaine and entering a recovery program, his mood improved significantly. Shannon, on the other hand, stopped drinking alcohol and using tranquilizers. The longer she was sober, however, the more anxious and depressed she became. Shannon was clearly suffering from psychiatric problems in addition to her dependence on substances. Her use of alcohol and tranquilizers was her way of coping with her symptoms through "self-medicating."

Homework

 ✎ Complete Self-Rating Scale.

Self-Rating Scale

Instructions: After reviewing your pattern of substance use and the consequences, rate the current severity of your problem. Then rate your current level of motivation to quit using substances and confidence level to maintain your sobriety.

Severity Level of My Problem

1	2	3	4	5	6	7
Mild		Moderate		Serious		Extremely Severe

My Motivation Level to Quit Using Substances

1	2	3	4	5	6	7
Definitely Don't Want to Quit		Some Desire to Quit		Strong Desire to Quit		Extremely Strong Desire to Quit

My Confidence in My Ability to Stay Sober

1	2	3	4	5	6	7
Low Confidence		Some Confidence		High Confidence		Very High Confidence

Chapter 3 — Recognizing Consequences of Your Substance Use

Goals

▪ To understand the consequences of your substance use and its effect on those close to you

▪ To identify problems caused by your substance abuse or dependence

Harmful Consequences

Substance use can contribute directly and indirectly to problems in any area of your life. Substance abuse and dependence raise the risk of medical, spiritual, psychological, psychiatric, family, and economic problems. Problems may range in severity from mild to life-threatening. Sometimes the effects are subtle or hidden. For example, an attorney with alcohol dependence initially reported that her work was not affected by her drinking. However, upon closer examination of her drinking patterns and functioning at work, she discovered that her billable hours had actually decreased by about 15% as her drinking worsened. A father of three with a tobacco dependence problem didn't think his children were too concerned about his smoking until they told him directly that they were upset, worried, and angry and felt he was cheating them by putting himself at risk for an early death due to smoking.

Effects of Substance Use Problems on the Family

Alcohol and drug problems often have a negative effect on the family. Loss of family relationships occurs due to separation, divorce, or involvement of child welfare agencies. Families feel neglected, and in some cases their basic needs for food, shelter, and clothing are ignored. The economic burden can be tremendous as a result of spending family income for drugs or alcohol, lost income due to impairment caused by substance use, and costs associated with legal, medical, or psychiatric problems. Family members often feel an emotional burden. Anger, fear, worry, distrust, and depression are common. Episodes of neglect, abuse, or violence are often associated with alcohol and other drug abuse. Substance abuse makes it difficult if not impossible to function responsibly as a parent or spouse, which leads to problems in family relationships. And due to the genetic predisposition associated with substance use disorder, children of parents who have these problems are more vulnerable than other children to developing their own substance use problems. These children therefore need all the help they can get to avoid developing a substance use problem.

Problems Associated With Substance Use Disorders

Table 3.1 summarizes of some of the more common problems associated with substance abuse and dependence, as reported in recent publications

Table 3.1 Problems Associated With Substance Use Disorders

Medical and Health: accidents; injuries; poor nutrition; weight gain or loss; poor personal hygiene; poor dental hygiene; increased risk of liver, heart, kidney, or lung diseases; cancers of the mouth or pharynx; gastritis; edema; high blood pressure; sexual dysfunction; complications with menstrual cycle, pregnancy, or childbirth; increased risk for sexually transmitted diseases, HIV, or AIDS; premature death

Emotional: anxiety; panic reactions; depression; mood swings; psychosis; feelings of anger or rage; suicidal thoughts, feelings, or behaviors; unpredictable behaviors; aggressiveness; violence; self-harm; feelings of shame and guilt; low self-esteem

Work/School: poor performance; lost jobs or dropping out of school; missing work or school; being undependable and less effective; loss of interest; ruined career; lost opportunities

Family: lost relationships due to separation, divorce, or involvement of child welfare agencies; family distress and conflict; damaged family relationships; emotional burden on the family (anger, hurt, distrust, fear, worry, depression); poor communication; perpetuation of substance use problems in children

Interpersonal Relationships: lost or damaged friendships; interpersonal conflicts and dissatisfaction; loss of trust or respect of significant others

Recreational: diminished interest in or loss of important hobbies, avocations, or other leisure activities

Legal: fines; legal constraints; arrests; convictions; jail or prison time; probation or parole

Economic: loss of income; excessive debts; falling behind in or ignoring financial obligations; loss of security or living arrangements; inability to take care of basic needs for food or shelter; using up all financial resources; inability to manage money

by the National Institutes of Health and based on our clinical experience. As you can see, these problems occur in all areas of functioning. After you've reviewed this chart and read the case examples that follow, complete the Harmful Effects Worksheet at the end of this chapter.

Case Examples

The following cases describe three individuals who sought treatment for problems with alcohol or other drugs. These cases clearly illustrate that the actual effects of the problems and level of motivation to quit vary significantly among individuals with alcohol or drug problems.

Tracy (Mild Effects)

Tracy is a 28-year-old, married, employed mother of two children who has a 6-year history of alcohol and marijuana abuse. Tracy is in good physical health and has had no major problems from her substance use. However, she reports that her occasional bouts of intoxication lead to arguments with her husband and that she feels guilty for embarrassing herself and her family. Tracy was also involved in a minor car accident while under the influence of marijuana. She has a fairly strong desire to quit using alcohol and marijuana because of these problems and her desire not to see things get worse.

Don (Moderate Effects)

Don is a 49-year-old college professor and married father of two adult children. He has had an alcohol problem for the past 10 years and has twice successfully completed rehabilitation programs, leading to periods of abstinence of several years. His most recent relapse came after 30 months of continuous sobriety. Although he is tenured at the college where he teaches, he feels pressure to maintain his sobriety because his last binge affected his ability to teach, and the dean of his department pressured him to seek professional help again. Don reports that his wife is worried about and upset with him, and his children are disappointed that he relapsed. He feels guilty and ashamed that he had to return to treatment after doing so well for several years. Don's latest relapse was also a factor in an episode of depression. Don's motivation to get back on track is very high. ▨

George (Severe Effects)

▨ *George is a 41-year-old, unemployed, divorced father of three children with a 23-history of alcoholism, heroin dependence, tobacco dependence, and crack cocaine abuse. George's wife left him over 15 years ago after he was arrested and spent time in jail for burglary. He became involved in crime at that time to support an expensive daily heroin addiction. Although George has not used any opiate drug in the past 11 years, his drinking has increased considerably. More recently, he has also started using crack cocaine. George states that his addiction has led to many serious problems in his life. These include losing several relationships with women; being a victim of a robbery and violent beatings on at least three occasions; getting kicked out of apartments many times, leading to periods of homelessness; poor nutrition, leading to loss of weight, dental problems, and poor physical health; gastritis caused by excessive drinking; gout; chronic obstructive pulmonary disease caused by excessive smoking; losing many jobs and being unable to work; and numerous arrests for public intoxication and for selling drugs. George has been in jail several times, hospitalized for complications of his alcoholism four times, hospitalized in a psychiatric facility twice following suicidal feelings after going on crack cocaine runs, detoxified in hospitals and Salvation Army social detoxification centers more than 20 times, and treated in addiction rehabilitation programs and halfway house programs at least five times. Although he once maintained continuous sobriety for over 2 years, the longest he has been able to stay sober in the past 5 years has been 3 months. George's desire to quit alcohol varies from one day to the next. Despite the severity of his addiction, he currently expresses only "some desire" to stop drinking alcohol.* ▨

Homework

✎ Complete Harmful Effects Worksheet.

Harmful Effects Worksheet

Problems Caused by or Worsened by Your Substance Use

Instructions: In the sections below, list any problems that you think were caused by or worsened by your alcohol, tobacco, or drug problem in the past year. Then, rank each of the eight categories from the most severe to the least severe, using "1" for the most severe category of problems.

Medical/physical/dental

2

Dental is not good. Fatty liver conditions

Psychological or emotional

1

Fairly severe depression and anxiety problems as a a result or cause of alcohol use and tranquilizer dependency

Work/school

3

See Economic

Family

4

Family and friends are concerned about excessive drinking

Interpersonal relationships

6

NO INTERPERSONAL PROBLEMS

Recreational

7

Didn't have have a great recreational life to begin with but have maintained most of what I did

Legal

8

NO LEGAL PROBLEMS

Economic

5

Economics stable but a premature bouts of panic attack and anxiety have caused me to retire earlier than planned

Change Issues and Strategies

Chapter 4 *Treatment Settings for Substance Use Problems*

Goals

▓ To learn the different levels of professional treatment for substance use problems

▓ To work closely with your therapist or counselor to figure out your specific goals and what steps you can take to reach them

Introduction

You should use the least restrictive level of professional treatment possible unless you have serious medical complications such as liver disease or gastritis, or serious psychiatric complications such as feeling suicidal, feeling persistently depressed, or feeling paranoid. The American Society of Addiction Medicine (ASAM) outlines levels of care for alcohol or other drug problems in a "stepped care" approach. The ASAM levels are listed below, from the least to most restrictive:

▓ Level 1: outpatient treatment

▓ Level 2: intensive outpatient treatment and partial hospitalization

▓ Level 3: medically monitored intensive inpatient treatment (residential)

▓ Level 4: medically managed intensive inpatient treatment (hospital)

The sections that follow describe the various types of treatment settings and provide some specific indicators for when each type of treatment is appropriate. Any questions you have regarding a particular level of treatment should be discussed with a therapist or a knowledgeable healthcare professional. If you try the least restrictive level of care and find that you are unable to establish and maintain abstinence from alcohol or other drugs, then you should consider a higher level of care and discuss it with your therapist or counselor.

Outpatient and Aftercare Programs (Level 1)

These programs vary in length from several weeks to months or longer. They may precede or follow detoxification or rehabilitation programs or be used as the sole treatment. Their purpose is to help people achieve and maintain abstinence or reduce harmful substance use, as well as to make personal changes to minimize relapse risk. Individual, group, and family therapy, medication management, and other ancillary services may be offered, depending on the specific setting. Outpatient treatment is most suitable if you are not at risk for withdrawal complications, have a stable medical and mental condition, show a willingness to cooperate with treatment, are able to maintain abstinence with minimal support, and have a supportive recovery environment. Outpatient treatment can also help you cope with your immediate environmental stresses.

Nonresidential Addiction Rehabilitation Programs (Level 2)

These short-term (2- to 6-week) programs include intensive outpatient and partial hospital programs. These programs provide addiction and recovery education and treatment and are appropriate if you do not need the supervision and structure of a residential or hospital-based program. These are sometimes used as "step-down" programs after someone has received treatment in a residential addiction program or hospital-based program, or as "step-up" programs when outpatient programs haven't helped someone get or stay sober. These programs are appropriate if you have a minimal withdrawal risk, have no serious medical conditions, have high enough resistance to recovery to require a structured treatment program, are likely to relapse without close monitoring and support, and have an unsupportive environment.

Inpatient Hospital and Residential Rehabilitation Programs (Levels 3 and 4)

These include both hospital-based and non–hospital-based residential programs. Some are "generic" in the sense that as long as someone meets the program's criteria, he or she can be admitted to the program. Others are highly specialized and serve specific populations based on type of and severity of addiction, gender, family status, or ethnicity. Following is a brief description of inpatient programs.

Short-Term Addiction Rehabilitation Programs

The traditional 28-day rehabilitation program has changed drastically. Most programs now offer a variable length of stay, with many clients staying less than 14 days. Unless you have serious medical or psychiatric problems, non–hospital-based programs are the first choice for rehabilitation. Addiction rehabilitation programs are recommended if you have been unable to get or stay sober through less intensive treatment settings such as outpatient, intensive outpatient, or partial hospital programs. They may also be used if your addiction is of such severity that a period of time in a structured, residential setting is needed to break the cycle of your addiction and help motivate you to establish a foundation for recovery. Short-term rehab programs are also appropriate if you have a high relapse potential, if your environment is considered dangerous for recovery, or if you do not have access to outpatient rehabilitation. Rehabilitation programs mainly focus on alcohol and drugs other than tobacco, although some are smoke-free or offer help if someone wants to quit smoking in addition to quitting use of other substances.

Long-Term Addiction Rehabilitation Programs

If you have a severe pattern of addiction and serious life impairment (e.g., no social support, lack of vocational skills, history of multiple relapses, serious problems with the legal system), you may need a long-term program. A long-term program can help you maintain sobriety by addressing some of the lifestyle and personality issues that you have to change to stay sober over time. Long-term rehab programs include therapeutic communities, halfway houses, and specialized programs dealing with specific populations such as men, women, women with children, specific ethnic groups, clients involved with the criminal justice system as a result of substance-related problems, and others. The trend is toward shorter-term programs. For example, therapeutic community programs that once were up to 2 years in length are now several months to less than a year in duration. Due to reduced government funding, fewer long-term programs are now available, and they are harder to get into than they were in the past.

Detoxification ("detox") refers to the process of tapering off substance use by using medicine to suppress or reduce withdrawal symptoms. Medical detoxification may be provided in an addiction rehabilitation facility, psychiatric hospital, or medical hospital. Medical detoxification is needed if you have a documented history of addiction, a significant potential for or current evidence of withdrawal complications such as seizures or delirium tremens (DTs) or serious suicidal feelings. A hospital-based program is appropriate if you have concurrent medical or psychiatric disorders that need to be monitored or managed while you detox. Detoxification normally takes up to several days. Detoxification from severe dependence on opiates or benzodiazepines may be started in a detox program and continued during ongoing outpatient or partial hospital treatment.

Some areas have "social detoxification" programs in which supportive care, rest, and nutrition are offered. Referrals are made to medical facilities in cases of complicated withdrawal. Social detox programs are usually provided for chronic substance abusers who have no medical insurance or way of paying for treatment. They are offered by organizations such as the Salvation Army.

Outpatient detoxification is appropriate if you have a less severe form of substance dependence, you don't show any evidence of serious medical or psychiatric problems, and you have support from family or other significant people. However, be aware that many clinics and doctors do not like to provide outpatient detoxification due to potential complications of withdrawal and to the fact that alcoholics and drug abusers may seek services for the wrong reasons.

Detoxification involves monitoring a person's vital signs and withdrawal symptoms. The detoxification process includes providing medications to prevent or stop physical withdrawal symptoms such as nausea, cramps, runny nose, sleep disturbance, anxiety, or agitation. Rest, nutrition, and evaluation of the person's physical and mental health are other components of detox. Detoxification has limited value if not followed by other treatments such as rehabilitation, outpatient care, or participation in self-help programs.

You should consider being detoxified under medical supervision if you:

- Cannot stop using alcohol or drugs on your own without jeopardizing your health

- Have a past history or current medical complications related to withdrawal or the effects of addiction (e.g., DTs, convulsions, elevated blood pressure, gastritis)

- Have a psychiatric disorder (e.g., psychotic symptoms, severe depression, suicidal feelings)

Withdrawal from alcohol or barbiturates is the most dangerous from a medical standpoint. Therefore, it is best that you be evaluated for supervised detoxification rather than quit on your own if you are dependent on these substances. Quitting "cold turkey" can produce serious medical or psychiatric complications, or the discomfort of withdrawal can cause you to continue to use substances to self-medicate your symptoms.

Special Programs

Other specialized treatment programs include those designed for smoking cessation, those designed as part of a treatment-research protocol to study specific types of outpatient psychosocial treatment (e.g., coping skills training or relapse prevention) or medication treatment, or those designed for people with dual or co-occurring disorders (substance use and psychiatric disorders).

Opiate Maintenance Therapy

Methadone maintenance (MM) is used to help opiate addicts who have been unsuccessful in their attempts to stop using opiate drugs. Provided in conjunction with education and counseling services, MM is designed to gradually wean someone from opiates altogether. A person may remain on MM for months or years. MM helps stop the use of illicit opiates and related criminal behavior and helps recovering individuals function at work and in the community. MM is a helpful treatment if you have been unable to stay off heroin or other opiate drugs despite being involved in other forms of treatment.

Buprenorphine (Subutex, Suboxone) is a newer medication used to help opiate addicts withdraw from drugs or maintain abstinence over time. It is being used more and more by addiction treatment programs and physicians but is not available in all treatment clinics because it requires a special license from the government. The advantage of buprenorphine over other opiate replacement drugs like methadone is that it can be prescribed by office-based physicians rather than being required to be dispensed through a treatment center. The potential for dependence on it is low, and it has a high safety profile. The sublingual form, Suboxone, has little street value and discourages intravenous use with a needle.

Choosing Your Goals

Your goals should be based on the severity of your current substance use problem, your motivation to change, and what you want to change about yourself and your lifestyle.

If you are in treatment, you should work closely with your therapist or counselor to figure out your specific goals and what steps you can take to reach them. There may be times when your therapist doesn't agree with your goals. For example, if you have alcohol dependence and choose the goal of moderating your drinking, your therapist will advise you to work toward abstinence because moderation is not appropriate goal for you. Or, if you agree to the goal of stopping heroin and cocaine use but still want to get high on alcohol or marijuana, your therapist will probably advise you to work toward total abstinence, because alcohol or marijuana use puts you at risk of returning to heroin and cocaine use.

If you are not sure what goals you want to set for yourself, then your initial goal can be "deciding what I want to change about myself and my alcohol, tobacco, or drug problem." The information in this workbook can help you in that process.

Homework

 ✎ Complete Initial Goals for Treatment Worksheet.

Initial Goals for Treatment Worksheet

1. Describe your primary goal for treatment at this time. _To WITHDRAW - DETOX FROM Alchohol and Antwan. I have psychatric issues involved - depression and anxiety. I believe I need supervised withdrawel care and post care for alchohol abstemence_

2. Describe what specific types of treatment you think you need at this time to reach your goal. ___ _detox for alchohol, detox for ATIVAN. 12 step program_

3. If you have been in treatment before, describe how it helped you. _18 years ago, detoxed from alchohol remained Sober for a year_

4. What can you do if you feel like leaving treatment before finishing it? _ask for help. Ask for medication_

Chapter 5   *Stages of Change*

Goals

▪ To learn the different stages you may go through as you recover from your substance use problem

▪ To identify the immediate and long-term consequences of either quitting or continuing to use substances

▪ To learn strategies to increase your motivation

Research studies have identified different stages that you may go through as you change a substance use problem. Although separated for purposes of discussion, you won't necessarily go through all of these stages or go through them in an orderly fashion. It isn't unusual to take two steps forward and one step back when changing your alcohol or drug problem. You may get stuck in one stage for a while, go back and forth between stages, or revisit an early stage of change after you have progressed to a later stage. Read about Prochaska, Norcross, and DiClemente's stages of change in Table 5–1, and then complete the Assessing Your Stage of Change Worksheet.

Strategies to Develop Your Motivation

One way to help you accept your problem and develop motivation is to review your Harmful Effects Worksheet (see Chapter 3). Another way is to complete the Decision-Making Matrix found at the end of this chapter. The information from these two exercises will help you look at both sides of the issue—quitting or continuing to use. It will help you clarify immediate and long-term consequences. Don't be surprised if you discover that you can make a strong case for continuing to use substances as well as a strong case for quitting. It's not a black-and-white issue that is easily resolved, because no matter what problems your alcohol or drug use has caused, you have gained something from using. At first, most people are ambivalent about totally quitting: part of them wants to quit and another part wants to continue drinking or using drugs. Your job is this: Look at all

Table 5.1 Stages of Change

1. The first stage of changing a substance problem, called *precontemplation,* is one in which you aren't aware of your problem. You are resistant to change because you don't think you have a problem. You are in denial and cannot see your alcohol or drug problem even if other people can.

2. The second stage is called *contemplation.* During this stage you acknowledge that you have a problem with alcohol or drugs, and you plan to take action within the next 6 months or so.

3. *Preparation,* the next stage, involves planning to do something about your alcohol or drug problem within the next month. You usually let others know about the change you are going to make. Even though you want to change, you still have mixed feelings about it—part of you wants to quit using alcohol or drugs, and part of you doesn't. Don't expect your motivation to be 100% at this point in the change process. You begin to think about the advantages of change.

4. The next stage, *action,* involves actually changing your alcohol or drug problem. You make a commitment to stop drinking alcohol, smoking, or using drugs. If you are physically addicted and cannot stop using on your own, or if you have a history of complications associated with stopping (e.g., seizure or suicidal thoughts or feelings), you should consider detoxification or hospitalization to help you stop using. In addition to getting sober or clean, during this stage you being to learn more about yourself so that you can also change your thinking, emotions, and self-image. You learn that coping with your substance use problem requires a lot more than simply stopping your use. You address the "nuts and bolts" issues of recovery, such as coping with thoughts about and cravings for substances; dealing with people, places, and things that can influence you to use again; coping with upsetting feelings; and dealing with family and relationship problems. You become involved in self-help groups or other forms of social support to build structure into your life, reduce boredom, and help you stay connected to others who care about your recovery.

5. *Maintenance,* or relapse prevention, is the next stage of change. During this stage, you continue to make positive changes in yourself and in your lifestyle. You work hard to prevent a return to alcohol or drug use and accept that there are no easy or quick solutions to your substance use problem. You learn to identify and manage relapse warning signs and high-risk situations. You work on balancing the various areas of your life so that you increase your chances of feeling good about yourself.

6. The final stage of change is called *termination.* In this stage, your former substance use problem no longer presents a temptation or threat. Your "old" behavior doesn't return and you have the confidence and skills to cope with your life problems so that the risk of relapsing to alcohol or drugs is low.

Adapted from Prochaska, J.O., Norcross, J.C., & DiClemente, C.C. (1994). *Changing for good.* New York: William Morrow.

sides of the issue, figure out the pros and cons of quitting, and work toward making a stronger case for quitting.

If your motivation wavers after you've been in recovery awhile, try to figure out what is happening at that time. Share your feelings and experiences with your therapist, an AA or NA sponsor or other members of support groups, or a confidant whom you trust with your inner feelings. Also, consider the following strategies to raise your motivation:

- Renew your commitment to recovery by reviewing your reasons for quitting alcohol or drug use.

- Remind yourself that low motivation is a temporary situation and things can change in the future.

- Review the benefits you have experienced in your recovery so far.

- Identify additional benefits from continued participation in recovery.

- Remember the problems caused by your use of alcohol or other drugs.

- Think about your children or other important people in your life and what your recovery means to them.

- Ask for input from others in recovery to find out what they did during periods of low motivation.

Homework

✎ Complete the Assessing Your Stage of Change Worksheet.

✎ Review the Harmful Effects Worksheet you completed in Chapter 3.

✎ Complete the Decision-Making Matrix.

Assessing Your Stage of Change Worksheet

Answer the following questions to help you determine where you are in your change process. Remember, progress is any movement through one stage to the next. Aim for change, not perfection! Place a check mark (√) in the appropriate box for each question.

	Absolutely Yes	Probably	Not Sure	Absolutely Not
Precontemplation/contemplation stages				
1. Do you think you have a problem with alcohol, tobacco, or other drugs?	☒	☐	☐	☐
2. Are you clear about why you want to quit using substances?	☒	☐	☐	☐
Preparation stage				
3. Are you willing to make a commitment to quit using within the next month?	☒	☐	☐	☐
4. Do you know what steps to take to stop using on your own?	☐	☐	☒	☐
5. Do you need to be detoxified from alcohol or other drugs to stop using?	☒	☐	☐	☐
6. Have you told others (family, friends, etc.) about your desire to change your problem with alcohol or other drugs?	☒	☐	☐	☐
Action stage				
7. Do you have a strong commitment to quit alcohol or drugs and stay sober?	☒	☐	☐	☐
8. Do you need to change people, places, or things to help you stay sober?	☐	☒	☐	☐
9. Do you need to learn to control your thoughts and cravings for substances?	☒	☐	☐	☐
10. Do you need to address the effects of your substance use on your family or other relationships to increase your chances of staying sober?	☐	☒	☐	☐
11. Do you need to address new ways of dealing with upsetting feelings to increase your chances of staying sober?	☒	☐	☐	☐
12. Are you willing to participate in self-help groups or other forms of social support to increase your chances of staying sober?	☒	☐	☐	☐

continued

	Absolutely Yes	Probably	Not Sure	Absolutely Not
Maintenance stage				
13. Do you know the warning signs of a potential relapse and have strategies to help you cope with these **before** you use alcohol, tobacco, or other drugs again?	☐	☐	☒	☐
14. Do you know your personal high-risk factors that make you feel vulnerable to using substances and have strategies to cope with these?	☐	☐	☐	☒
15. Do you know what steps to take should you actually go back to using substances following a period of abstinence?	☐	☒	☐	☐
16. Is your life generally in balance?	☐	☐	☐	☒

There are no questions about the termination phase because we assume that you would not need this workbook if you were in that phase of change.

Decision-Making Matrix: Pros and cons of quitting

Instructions: In the sections below, write the pros and cons of quitting and of continuing to use alcohol, tobacco, or other drugs. Provide examples of both immediate and long-term consequences of each decision.

To stop using or remain abstinent

Immediate consequences		Long-term consequences	
Positive	**Negative**	**Positive**	**Negative**
Save my liver	lose my health	Stay healthy, happy	Spend out of control ~~Spend~~.

To continue using

Immediate consequences		Long-term consequences	
Positive	**Negative**	**Positive**	**Negative**
feel good, stable nervous relief	ruining my health job or retirement instability	Nothing	Shorten life lose relationships

Chapter 6   *How to Use Therapy or Counseling*

Goals

- To learn to get the most out of your treatment

- To familiarize yourself with those behaviors that may have a negative impact on your therapy

Introduction

There are many different types of therapy and counseling approaches for alcohol, tobacco, and other drug problems. Research shows that there is no single, superior treatment approach. Professional treatment is most effective when it helps you to develop and improve skills for dealing with the many challenges and demands of recovery and the problems associated with your substance use. Involving your family in the treatment process can also raise the chances of successful treatment; so can active participation in mutual support groups such as AA or NA.

Usually, the more severe your substance use problem, the more time you need in treatment to gain maximum benefit. For less severe substance use problems, short-term outpatient treatment consisting of fewer than 12 sessions is often effective. For dependency problems, longer time in outpatient treatment is needed. In some instances, detoxification and/or residential treatment may have to precede outpatient therapy.

Getting the Most out of Treatment

To increase the chances for recovery, certain attitudes have proved helpful. Recovery is more about change in yourself—attitudes, values, behaviors, and personality—than it is about alcohol or drugs. In fact, only step 1 of the 12 steps of AA and NA mentions the term "alcohol or addiction." The steps address you, the person, not the substance. Here are some ideas to help you get the most out of your treatment and involvement in recovery:

- *Share your story and history.* It is best to be honest in sharing the details of your personal story of substance use so that the professionals assessing you have a true picture of your problem and you. This will enable them to make recommendations for your treatment and recovery plan. Sharing your story and history honestly in group therapy sessions and AA or NA meetings is also helpful in recovery. You can get support, advice, and feedback from others in recovery from an alcohol or drug problem.

- *Develop a trusting relationship with a therapist or counselor.* This is essential in getting the most out of treatment. Let your therapist or counselor know what bothers you, what goes well, what you like and dislike about your work together, and your problems. Make sure you share the truth about close calls, substance cravings, actual episodes of alcohol or drug use, high-risk situations, or motivational struggles.

- *Keep your appointments.* Keep your appointments and stay in treatment long enough to reap the benefits. Do not create excuses and leave treatment against the advice of the people providing your care. Dropping out early is usually a bad sign and often precedes relapse. Be honest and open up in your sessions. Do not keep secrets, especially if you relapse. Your counselor is there to help you, not judge you. Follow through with the agreements you make with your counselor or treatment group. It is up to you to follow your treatment plan and take action to change.

- *Stay long enough to benefit from treatment.* Treatment is effective to the extent that you stay long enough to benefit from it. For many, alcohol or drug dependence is a long-term, chronic condition that often requires you to stay in treatment for months or longer. Many choose to stay in support groups like AA or NA for years.

- *Get help with motivation when it is low.* Your motivation to stay sober may go up and down in the early months of sobriety. You can feel enthusiastic one day, then negative about recovery the next day. You may work hard at your change plan only to find yourself feeling less motivated.

- *Accept that recovery is ongoing.* You will always have to actively work on not using alcohol or drugs and being aware of your problem. Since your problem developed over time, it will not easily or quickly be overcome. Recovery happens gradually, often in small steps. Many people in AA or NA have been involved in these programs for years. They know recovery continues long after they stop using alcohol or other drugs. There are no short cuts. Those who expect quick fixes set themselves up for failure.

- *Acknowledge that recovery can be painful.* It requires an open and honest look at life in relation to alcohol and drug use, and how this use has affected you and others. This self-examination may evoke guilt, shame, anger, and disappointment. As recovery progresses and changes are made, the pain decreases.

- *Accept abstinence as your goal.* It is best to accept abstinence as a goal since it is common to transfer addictions or accumulate new ones. The need for abstinence is stressed in self-help programs and in their literature. The "basic text" of NA states in the opening chapter that "we [addicts] could not successfully use any mind-altering or mood-changing substance." This book, written by recovering drug addicts, also points out how easy it is for an addict to justify legal prescriptions and cautions the addict who may need some type of mood-altering substance. This problem is also discussed in books written for recovering alcoholics. An entire chapter is devoted to "avoiding chemical mood changers" in the book *Living Sober: Some Methods AA Members Have Used for Not Drinking.* Even if it takes you time to work toward abstinence, this is a step in the right direction, as not everyone is able or willing to accept abstinence at first.

- *Make changes in yourself.* Making changes in yourself or your lifestyle is the real challenge of recovery. These changes may relate to thinking patterns, how emotions are handled, how problems are solved, relationships to others, how and where free time is used, and self-image. Your change plan should be based on your problems and what you want to see different in your life.

■ *Consider medications.* Medications are used to help people safely withdrawal from addictive substances, to help with their ongoing recovery, as replacements for substances to which they became physically addicted (e.g., methadone or buprenorphine as a substitute for heroin), or for treatment of co-occurring medical or psychiatric disorders (e.g., antidepressants for depression or mood stabilizers for bipolar illness). If you have trouble staying sober with therapy or counseling alone, ask your therapist to schedule a medication evaluation.

■ *Improve your coping skills.* Learning coping skills to deal with problems resulting from or contributing to substance use disorders is critical for your long-term success. You may need help in developing cognitive, behavioral, and interpersonal skills to deal with a range of recovery challenges (e.g., setting goals, managing cravings, managing upsetting feelings, dealing with interpersonal conflict, resisting pressures to engage in substance use behavior, identifying and managing early warning signs of relapse and high-risk factors; see Chapters 7 to 18) or managing co-occurring psychiatric disorders (see Chapter 20). Developing coping skills involves education, awareness, practice and more practice, and the ability to try new things to cope.

■ *Address family issues.* Since substance use disorders affect the family, discuss with your counselor the impact of your substance use on your family, how to improve family communication and relationships, and what treatment and self-help services can benefit your family (e.g., counseling, Al-Anon or Nar-Anon meetings). Involving your family is often helpful to both you and your family (see Chapter 12): you get support from them, and they get a chance to share their story and receive help and support. When families are involved in treatment, the outcome often improves.

■ *Expand your recovery network.* A supportive social network consisting of family, friends, and others in recovery who care about your well-being can help you recover in many ways (see Chapters 13 and 14). Work with your counselor to identify new sources of support so you have a larger recovery network to depend on. If you have difficulty asking others for help or support, work with your counselor to learn ways to reach out and ask others for their support.

- *Attend AA, NA, DRA, Rational Recovery, SMART Recovery, Women for Sobriety, or other mutual support group meetings.* Open up and share your problems and struggles with your sponsor or friends in any of these mutual support groups. Learn to ask others with similar problems for their help and support. For example, sharing openly with another member of a support group your strong desire to use alcohol or drugs or a decrease in your motivation to change can help you figure out what to do to maintain your sobriety. Go to meetings regularly, especially in the early months of recovery. Participate in meetings by sharing and asking questions. Do not worry about being judged for anything you share or how you think, because others with alcohol or drug problems like yours know how hard it can be to change at times or how motivation wavers.

- *Get help with any psychiatric problem.* Psychiatric disorders are common among individuals with substance use disorders (see Chapter 20). If you think you may have a problem, ask for an evaluation by a mental health professional.

- *Prepare for lapse and relapse.* Learning to spot early warning signs of relapse and take action and identifying your potential high-risk situations can help you reduce your risk of relapse (see Chapters 18 and 19). Since you may not experience a straight path in your recovery, prepare for setbacks and emergencies so you have a plan to quickly address any return to substance use or any problem or behavior that you think can lead you back to using alcohol or drugs.

- *Review your progress frequently, especially in early recovery.* There are a variety of ways to check your progress (see Chapter 19). Are you following your plan to change? Are you using active coping skills to manage the challenges of recovery? Are you able to stop your substance use? Are you able to fight through periods of low motivation to change? Are you making improvements in yourself (how you think, feel, or act) or your life? Progress is not an "all or none" issue and should be measured relative to your problems and treatment goals. Your progress is affected by the severity of your problem, your motivation, and your personal resources.

Difficulty Asking for Help

Pride, fear, embarrassment, worry, and not knowing how can get in the way of asking for help from others. View recovery as a "we" rather than an "I" effort in which you ask others for help or support when you need it. This can happen on many levels: you need a ride to a meeting; you need advice on how to handle a problem; you need someone to listen to your concerns; or you need someone to talk with about something important. You can seek help or support related to any area of life—your health, emotions, relationships, spirituality, finances, or work. Be direct in your request and try to be as specific as you can in terms of what kind of help and support you need from others. Then, be gracious in accepting the help or support offered. Following are some ideas on how to ask for and use help from others:

- Face your fears or reluctance to ask for help and support from others.

- Have a list of people (and phone numbers) you can rely on for help or support.

- Share your concerns and feelings with at least one or two confidants (people you trust).

- Take risks in opening up and sharing with others.

- Join a mutual support program (AA, NA, DRA, or mental health group) and get involved in the program.

Leaving Treatment Early or Against Medical Advice

Some people stop partial hospital, intensive outpatient, or outpatient treatment before finishing their program or course of counseling. Others leave hospital detoxification or rehabilitation programs against medical advice (AMA). The reasons they give for leaving treatment early or AMA are usually smokescreens and not the real reason: the real reason usually relates to a desire to use alcohol or drugs again or lower motivation to finish treatment.

One of the features of addiction that contributes to a decision to quit treatment or leave AMA is a "covert" craving. This means that on some level you desire or crave alcohol or drugs, but you attribute your desire to quit treatment to another reason (e.g., you don't like the treatment you're getting, you're not getting the medicine you want, you don't like the staff, you think you know everything taught by the counseling or medical staff, you feel anxious or irritable, or you have some personal business to attend to).

Addiction affects your thinking, emotions, and ability to make decisions in your best interest. If you accept your addiction as an illness or disease and accept that your treatment team or counselor knows more than you about what is in your best interest, you can prevent yourself from quitting treatment early or leaving AMA.

If you leave AMA, your risk of relapse is high. Many people who quit treatment or leave a detox or rehab program use alcohol or drugs right away. It is OK if you want to quit or leave treatment early—just don't do it. Instead, put your desire into words and talk with your counselor, nurse, doctor, any other professional involved in your care, an AA or NA sponsor if you have one, or trusted friend or confidant. Sometimes simply putting your desires and problems into words gives these less control over you. If you talk about your addiction, cravings to use, and desire to leave treatment, you may gain a fresh view of what is happening.

Treatment Outcome

Many studies show that treatment of substance use disorders is effective, especially if you stay long enough to reap the benefit of it. These positive effects of professional help may include:

- Improved rates of engagement, or getting involved in treatment

- Improved rates of following your treatment plan and attending your sessions

- Improved rates of completing treatment

- Stopping substance use

- Cutting down on the frequency and amount of substances used

- Improved physical health

- Improved mental health

- Improved spiritual health

- Improved family relationships

- Increased satisfaction with marriage

- Improved social behaviors (e.g., fewer problems with the law, improved employment rates, less dependence on welfare)

Behaviors That Interfere With the Effectiveness of Therapy

Therapy-sabotaging behaviors interfere with getting the most from your counseling or therapy sessions. Being familiar with these behaviors puts you in a position to take action if you experience them. Complete the Therapy-Sabotaging Behavior Worksheet. This worksheet will help you identify behaviors that can impede your progress. After identifying those behaviors you have experienced, you should think about methods of handling each behavior without letting it sabotage your counseling.

Homework

✎ Complete the Therapy-Sabotaging Behavior Worksheet.

✎ Complete the Past Treatment Experiences Worksheet.

Therapy-Sabotaging Behavior Worksheet

Instructions: Review each behavior below. Place a check mark (√) next to it if you've ever experienced it in relation to your therapy or counseling. Then, choose two behaviors you have experienced and develop an action plan for coping with each behavior.

___ Not attending my sessions on time
___ Skipping my session entirely
___ Missing sessions because I was upset with my counselor
___ Dropping out of counseling after only a few sessions
___ Not following through and completing assignments or journal exercises between my counseling sessions
___ Blaming my counselor for not helping me enough
___ Talking about how to change in my sessions but not actually translating these changes into my life
___ Expecting my counselor to solve my problems.
___ Expecting my counselor to tell me what to talk about in my sessions
___ Not opening up and telling my counselor what I really think or feel

___ Not telling my counselor when I feel like using substances or have actually used between sessions
___ Constantly calling my counselor on the phone or leaving messages
___ Placing unrealistic demands on my counselor
___ Not properly taking medications such as Antabuse® or naltrexone, or medications for a concurrent psychiatric disorder
___ Not accepting responsibility for those things over which I have control
___ Not accepting responsibility for _____ (things over which I have influence)
___ Blaming others for my behavior choices
___ Placing myself in high-risk situations

Behavior 1: _____

_____

Action Plan: _____

_____

_____

_____

_____

Behavior 2: _____

_____

Action Plan: _____

_____

_____

_____

_____

Review of Your Past Treatment Experiences Worksheet

Check the following types of treatment you have received in the past for your addiction. For each item you check under "treatment programs and counseling or therapy," write in the number of different times you received this treatment during your lifetime. For each "Medication" you have used, write in how long you took this medication.

Treatment Programs and Counseling or Therapy

☐ Detoxification: # of times _____

☐ Residential or hospital-based rehab (less than 30 days): # of times _____

☐ Residential or hospital-based rehab (more than 30 days): # of times _____

☐ Halfway House: # of times _____

☐ Therapeutic Community: # of times _____

☐ Partial Hospital or Day Treatment Program: # of times _____

☐ Intensive Outpatient Program: # of times _____

☐ Outpatient Counseling: # of times _____

☐ Program for Women: # of times _____

☐ Program for Dual Diagnosis (Addiction + Mental Illness): # of times _____

☐ Specialty Program for Criminal Justice Problems: # of times _____

Medications for Addiction

☐ Methadone Maintenance (for opiate addiction): how long? _____

☐ Buprenorphine (subutex and suboxone for opiate addiction): how long? _____

☐ Disulfiram (Antabuse for alcoholism): how long? _____

☐ Naltrexone (ReVia for alcoholism): how long? _____

☐ Naltrexone (Trexan for opioid addiction): how long? _____

☐ Acamprosate (Campral for alcoholism): how long? _____

1. How many different times have you left detoxification, hospital, or residential based treatment against medical advice?

    ☐ 0 ☐ 1 ☐ 2 ☐ 3 ☐ 4 ☐ 5 ☐ over 5

2. How many different times have you stopped partial hospital, intensive outpatient, or outpatient treatment before it was finished?

    ☐ 0 ☐ 1 ☐ 2 ☐ 3 ☐ 4 ☐ 5 ☐ over 5

3. Overall, how would you rate your personal investment in treatment *in the past?*

    ☐ None   ☐ Low   ☐ Moderate   ☐ High

4. Overall, how would you rate your personal investment in treatment *at the present?*

    ☐ None   ☐ Low   ☐ Moderate   ☐ High

5. Describe how treatment helped you in the past. Be as specific and detailed as you can.

6. If you dropped out of treatment early in the past, or left a program against medical advice, describe the effects of this (on your alcohol and drug use; your health; your relationships; and other areas of your life).

7. What could you do to help yourself if you begin thinking about missing your sessions, dropping out of treatment, or leaving a program against medical advice?

Chapter 7 | *Overview of Goal Planning*

Goals

▨ To begin to set and prioritize your recovery goals

▨ To learn about the different components of recovery

Introduction

Recovery is a process in which you set goals to work toward stopping substance use and learn skills to change yourself and your lifestyle so you can live substance-free. Recovery goal planning involves:

▨ Becoming educated about your specific type of substance use problem (e.g., medical effects, consequences of continued use, treatments)

▨ Developing a desire to change

▨ Meeting the demands and challenges of recovery

▨ Setting specific goals for change

▨ Developing action plans to help you change and developing a relapse plan to help you maintain changes

Strengthening your existing coping skills and learning new skills to meet the demands of recovery are essential for long-term change.

Your recovery plan may address one or several domains of recovery: physical, emotional or psychological, family, social or interpersonal, spiritual, or lifestyle. The specific goals you choose are personal, based on how you see your substance use problem and what you believe you need to change about yourself and your lifestyle. When you finish reading this chapter, complete the Goal-Planning Worksheet. This will help you begin to set goals and develop action plans to reach them. You can come back and add to your Goal-Planning Worksheet later, after you have reviewed additional sections of this workbook. You may photocopy the worksheet from this book or download additional copies at the Treatments That Work™ website at http://www.oup.com/us/ttw. You can revisit this issue after you've completed all the sections of this workbook that you think pertain to you. Remember, goal planning is an ongoing process: you are always going to be working toward goals and making changes in yourself and in your lifestyle.

Physical Recovery

The physical component of recovery includes:

▦ Getting alcohol- or drug-free

▦ Taking care of physical problems resulting from or worsened by your substance use

▦ Eating a balanced diet to ensure proper nutrition

▦ Getting sufficient sleep, rest, and relaxation to reduce stress and help increase your energy

▦ Exercising regularly to maintain good physical health and reduce stress

▦ Learning to manage physical craving to use substances

Stopping substance use offers an excellent opportunity to be more health-conscious and to take better care of your body.

Emotional or Psychological Recovery

This component of recovery includes:

▦ Accepting that you have a problem and making a commitment to do something about it

▦ Learning to challenge negative thinking that can lead you back to substance use

▦ Learning to cope with upset feelings, stress, and life problems without resorting to using alcohol, tobacco, or other drugs for relief or escape

If you have a coexisting psychiatric disorder or a psychological problem, you will need to address this as well to increase your chances of staying sober. However, you need to be careful about attempting to deal with too many issues too soon in the recovery process. Therefore, we advise you to wait until you've had a substantial period of sobriety (at least several months) before attempting to deal with any deep-seated emotional problem such as being a victim of physical, sexual, or psychological abuse. The exception is developing a safety plan if you are currently in an abusive relationship or you feel seriously depressed, hopeless, suicidal, or concerned that you might harm someone else. If your psychiatric symptoms are causing significant personal distress or impairment in your life, you may need to address these (see Chapter 20).

Family Recovery

Because loved ones are usually affected in one way or another by substance use problems, it helps to examine how your problem has affected your family. Then you can decide what you can do to improve your relationships with family members. Often, it is helpful to invite them to attend therapy session, education groups, or "open" AA or NA meetings. You can also encourage your family to attend support groups such as Al-Anon or Nar-Anon. Taking a close look at your problem's impact on your family may temporarily contribute to feelings of guilt and shame. In the long run, however, you put yourself in a better position to develop stronger family ties.

Social or Interpersonal Recovery

Personal relationships and leisure interests are frequently damaged by substance use problems. You may have to make amends to others hurt by your substance use, rebuild damaged relationships, make new friends with others who do not get high, learn to assertively refuse offers to use, and develop healthy leisure interests to replace time spent using substances. If you have a long-standing addiction, you may have to learn to have fun again and find new leisure activities that provide you with a sense of enjoyment and fulfillment.

Spiritual Recovery

This domain of recovery refers to overcoming the feelings of shame and guilt that often accompany a substance use problem. Shame refers to feeling bad about yourself, like you are defective or weak. Guilt refers to feeling bad about the things that you did or failed to do when using substances. For some, developing a sense of meaning in life is an important component of their spiritual recovery. Belief in a higher power and participation in formal religion are two common ways in which people work on their personal spirituality. As recovery progresses, some find it helpful to "give back" to others suffering from similar problems. Some self-help programs such as Rational Recovery (RR) do not believe in the need for a relationship with a higher power for a successful recovery. Therefore, you may receive conflicting viewpoints on the issue of spirituality in recovery; only you can decide what works for you. Also, many people interpret spirituality from a broad perspective that goes beyond belief in following a specific religion or belief in a higher power. Mindfulness and meditation, for example, are common disciplines used to get in touch with one's inner self.

Other Areas of Recovery

Areas such as work, school, hobbies, legal issues, exercise, money, or creativity may also need to be addressed in your change plan. For example, if your substance use has caused problems with your job or significant financial problems, you need to deal with these. Information about lifestyle balance is presented in Chapter 18. This information can help you plan goals related to these other areas of recovery.

Prioritizing Your Goals

In addition to having specific recovery goals, you have to set priorities. This involves working on the most pressing issues first. You can sabotage your progress if you work on late recovery issues while ignoring early recovery issues. For example, Darren's drug dependence wreaked havoc on his family, causing his parents to feel worried, angry, and at their wit's end about how to help him. His dependency also damaged many of his other relationships. So that he could eventually try to fix some of the relationship damage, Darren first had to sustain his abstinence and learn to manage his constant cravings to get high. His initial goal was to get totally off drugs. This was followed by learning to manage his cravings and find healthy social support. After he took care of these critical issues, he was in better psychological shape to begin working on developing better relationships.

If you will not or cannot get totally off alcohol or drugs as the first step, think about what steps you can take to move toward change, rather than doing nothing at all and letting your problem get worse. The very worst thing you can do is nothing at all. If you start the process now, even if you fight within yourself over whether or not to stop completely, at least you can give yourself a chance to make this decision later. It's OK to admit you don't yet know if you want to change. Use the information in this workbook to help you decide if you want to change your substance use problem.

Homework

 ✎ Complete the Goal-Planning Worksheet.

Goal-Planning Worksheet

Instructions: For each domain of recovery, list any changes you want to make. For each change that you identify, write the steps you can take to help you achieve your goal. Try to be as concrete as you can in identifying your goals and your change strategies.

Change	Goal	Steps toward change
Physical		
Emotional or phychological		
Family		
Social or interpersonal		
Spiritual		
Other (work, economic, etc.)		

Chapter 8

Managing Cravings and Urges to Use Substances

Goals

▓ To learn strategies that will help you prevent or manage your cravings

▓ To begin tracking your cravings on a daily basis over the next few months

▓ To identify the things that trigger your cravings in order to plan coping strategies

Introduction

A *craving* is a longing for or a desire to use a substance that varies in intensity from mild to very strong. Your craving can be a desire for the euphoric high associated with using substances, or it can be a desire to avoid or escape unpleasant moods or physical symptoms such as those associated with withdrawal.

An *urge* is your intention to use substances once you have a craving. You can have a strong craving with very little intention to use, or your intention to use can be quite high, making you more vulnerable to relapse unless you use active coping strategies to help you through your craving and urge.

Cravings can be overt so that you are aware of them, or they can be covert (hidden from your awareness) and show up in indirect ways such as irritability. Cravings tend to be more frequent and stronger in the early days and weeks of recovery.

Cravings for substances are triggered by something external (people, places, events, experiences, or objects) or internal (feelings or thoughts). Your cravings vary in intensity from low to severe and in how they are manifested in your body. When you experience a craving, your thoughts and feelings determine how you cope with it. These connections are shown graphically in Figure 8.1 and discussed in further detail in this chapter.

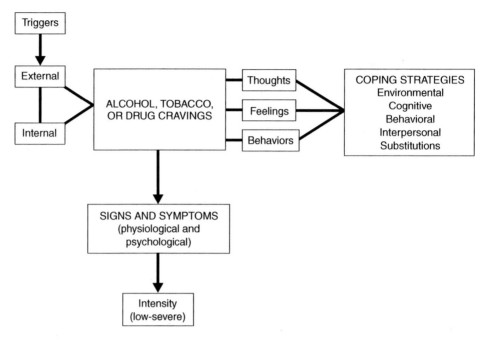

Figure 8.1 Craving triggers and intensities.

It takes a while to adjust to not using substances, both physically and mentally. It also takes time to figure out what triggers your cravings and to practice ways of managing them. The strategies reviewed in this chapter should help you prevent or manage your cravings.

Rating Your Cravings on a Daily Basis

Learning to identify and label your cravings is the first step toward controlling them. You can call them whatever feels comfortable—urge, craving, desire, need to get high, and so forth. When you start your recovery, it helps to track your cravings on a daily basis so that you can see how they change from day to day. It also helps to be aware of how cravings and urges manifest themselves in physiological and behavioral symptoms. Anxiety, tension, sweaty palms, racing heart, irritability, avoiding people, and lying to people are just a few common ways in which your cravings may show up. Use the Daily Craving Record to track your cravings over the next few months. You may photocopy the form from this book or download multiple copies from the Treatments That Work™ website at http://www.oup.com/

Daily Craving Record

Ratings of Intensity of Cravings

Instructions: Each day, use the scale to rate the average intensity (0–5) of your cravings to use alcohol, tobacco, or other drugs.

0	1	2	3	4	5
None	Low		Moderate		Severe

Month: _October_

Day	1	2	3	4	5	6	7	8	9	10	11	12	13	14	15	16
Rating	5	5	4	4	5	5	4	4	5	4	4	3	4	4	5	4
Day	17	18	19	20	21	22	23	24	25	26	27	28	29	30	31	
Rating	4	3	3	3	4	3	3	5	3	3	3	3	2	3	3	

Month: _November_

Day	1	2	3	4	5	6	7	8	9	10	11	12	13	14	15	16
Rating	3	3	2	4	3	3	3	2	2	3	3	3	3	3	3	5
Day	17	18	19	20	21	22	23	24	25	26	27	28	29	30	31	
Rating	3	2	3	3	3	3	2	2	3	2	3	3	3	3		

Month: _December_

Day	1	2	3	4	5	6	7	8	9	10	11	12	13	14	15	16
Rating	3	2	2	3	3	2	2	1	2	2	2	2	2	3	2	1
Day	17	18	19	20	21	22	23	24	25	26	27	28	29	30	31	
Rating	1	2	2	1	2	2	2	2	2							

Figure 8.2 Example of completed Daily Craving Record.

ttw/us. Take a few minutes at the end of each day and rate the average intensity of the cravings you had during the day, using a scale of 0 to 5; a rating of 0 indicates no cravings, 1 indicates low craving intensity, 3 indicates moderate craving intensity, and 5 indicates severe craving intensity. Because the first 90 days of recovery present the highest risk of relapse, we recommend that you track your cravings so you can see how the ratings change over time. If you abstain from substances, the intensity of your cravings will probably lessen as time goes on. However, there may be days during which you experience a temporary increase in your cravings. For example, Sharon's daily ratings were "severe" for the first 2 to 3 weeks and "moderate" to "severe" during the next 2 to 3 weeks. The intensity of her cravings decreased during the second and third months. About 6 weeks into her abstinence, she experienced severe cravings for a day. As with any increase in craving severity, the important issue is managing it without using. Eventually, all cravings go away or lessen in severity.

As you track your cravings and rate them on a daily basis, pay close attention to the internal and external triggers that you associate with them and the coping strategies you use to avoid taking a substance. For example, Sharon's cravings have recently increased. Sharon has been able to figure out a connection between upset feelings in a relationship and an increase in the severity of cravings. The next two sections will discuss the connection between your cravings, triggers, and coping strategies.

Identifying Triggers to Use Substances

Identifying the people, places, events, and situations that trigger your cravings or urges helps you anticipate triggers, which can in turn help you plan coping strategies.

External triggers include people, places, events, situations, or objects that directly or indirectly contribute to your desire to use substances. Common "people" triggers include drinking buddies, drug dealers, partners or roommates who use substances, or coworkers and friends who smoke in front of you. Any place where you previously used substances (e.g., home, office, bar, friend's house, street corner, car) can trigger a desire to use. Similarly, events or situations in which substances are being used can be a trigger for you. These include but are not limited to parties; holiday, religious, or personal celebrations; after-work get-togethers; or business meetings. Even objects can trigger your cravings. These include the sight or smell of alcohol, tobacco, or other drugs; the smell of a particular perfume or cologne; the sight of paraphernalia associated with using (e.g., lighters, mirrors, pipes, papers, needles, alcohol mixers); and the sight, smell, or experience of other objects associated with using. Ryan identified certain pieces of music as triggers for marijuana use. Even when he had no desire to use, if he heard particular songs while riding in the car, he would experience a craving for marijuana. Common triggers for smokers are a cup of coffee and the end of a good dinner, as these are often associated with using cigarettes.

Cravings and urges can also be triggered by internal factors such as feelings, specific thoughts or memories, or physical sensations. Distressing feelings such as anxiety, depression, or anger frequently trigger desires to use again. It takes time and effort to learn to manage feelings. Negative emotional states are the most common relapse risk factor. Therefore, learning skills to manage your feelings will reduce your vulnerability to relapse. Chapter 10 includes strategies for managing your upsetting feelings. Positive thoughts and memories of using can trigger cravings and urges as well. Examples include, "I really don't have a problem," "I can handle a few," "There's nothing like a few drinks (cigarettes, joints, lines of cocaine)," "I can't stand living without getting high on drugs," "Sex is so much better when I'm buzzed up."

Sometimes, cravings will be random and likely to happen at any given day or time. At other times, however, cravings may be more likely to happen during specific days or times. For example, when Dana first quit drinking, her cravings were like clockwork: as soon as the "cocktail" hour arrived, her desire for a few drinks before dinner increased. When she ate out in a nice restaurant, she associated having a few glasses of wine with enjoying a good meal.

Although we classify triggers as internal and external for purposes of discussion, they are often interrelated: an external trigger will lead to increased thoughts of using. However, it is not uncommon, especially in cases of substance dependency, to want to use substances solely because addiction has become part of you and need not be externally triggered.

After reading the rest of this chapter, complete the Substance Use Triggers Worksheet to help you identify triggers, the degree of threat each trigger represents, and strategies to help you cope with them. Helpful coping strategies are summarized in the following section.

When possible, it is best to choose a strategy that provides a substitute "payoff." For example, if you drank to relax and cope with stress, then you need an alternative way to relax and reduce stress. If you smoked marijuana or snorted cocaine to enhance sex, then you need to find ways to enjoy sex without relying on drugs. If you smoked cigarettes to quell your anger, then you need to find healthier ways of dealing with anger.

As you review the following coping strategies, place a check mark next to those you have successfully used in the past or can use in the future.

Environmental Coping Strategies

- Reduce environmental cues by getting rid of the substances you are trying to quit using. If you are quitting smoking or drinking, there is no need to keep cigarettes or alcohol in your house for other people.

- Get rid of paraphernalia used to prepare or ingest drugs (e.g., lighters, ashtrays, needles, mirrors, papers).

- In early recovery, when possible, avoid people, places, events, and things that you feel represent a high risk of relapse.

Cognitive Coping Strategies

- Talk yourself through the craving.

- Tell yourself that you are capable of coping with a craving no matter how strong it is.

- Remember that cravings always pass in time.

- Buy yourself time by saying you'll put off using for a few hours.

- Remember the troubles caused by using alcohol or other drugs.

- Ask for help and strength from a higher power.

- Imagine the craving as a wave that you are surfing to safety. Rather than fight against the wave, you ride it to shore without getting engulfed in it. "Ride out" the craving and it will eventually leave you.

- Delay your decision by telling yourself you'll wait until later in the day or tomorrow before you use. By that time, your desire may have decreased in intensity or left completely.

Behavioral Coping Strategies

- Distract yourself with an activity.

- Do something physical, such as take a walk, jog, or work out, to release tension.

- Write in a journal or complete a daily craving record (see http://www.stayingsober.lifejournal.com).

- Read recovery literature for help and inspiration.

Interpersonal Coping Strategies

- Talk to friends in recovery.

- Talk to family or other supportive people.

- Go to a self-help recovery meeting and share your cravings.

- Leave situations immediately if the pressure to use feels too strong to resist.

- Avoid interpersonal "set-ups." These are relationships or encounters that influence you to use. This influence may be overt or direct, or subtle and indirect. If, for example, you want to date someone who gets high on alcohol and drugs, or have a sexual encounter with someone who is drinking or using drugs, you may not initially feel like using. Later, your desire to use may increase as the situation unfolds and the person you are with invites you to use or uses in front of you.

Substitute Coping Strategies

- Smokers find it helpful to chew gum or eat mints or hard candy when they feel like having a cigarette.

- Substituting a soft drink or other non-alcoholic drink is helpful during times or situations associated with alcohol use, such as the pre-dinner cocktail hour.

Homework

✎ Use the Daily Craving Record to track your cravings over the next few months.

✎ Complete the Substance Use Triggers Worksheet to help you identify triggers, the degree of threat each trigger represents, and strategies to help you cope with them.

Daily Craving Record

Ratings of Intensity of Cravings

Instructions: Each day, use the scale to rate the average intensity (0–5) of your cravings to use alcohol, tobacco, or other drugs.

0 ——————— 1 ——————— 2 ——————— 3 ——————— 4 ——————— 5

None   Low   Moderate   Severe

Month: _____

Day	1	2	3	4	5	6	7	8	9	10	11	12	13	14	15	16
Rating																
Day	17	18	19	20	21	22	23	24	25	26	27	28	29	30	31	
Rating																

Month: _____

Day	1	2	3	4	5	6	7	8	9	10	11	12	13	14	15	16
Rating																
Day	17	18	19	20	21	22	23	24	25	26	27	28	29	30	31	
Rating																

Month: _____

Day	1	2	3	4	5	6	7	8	9	10	11	12	13	14	15	16
Rating																
Day	17	18	19	20	21	22	23	24	25	26	27	28	29	30	31	
Rating																

Substance Use Triggers Worksheet

Instructions: List people, places, events, situations, objects, feelings, thoughts, memories, or times of day that trigger your cravings or urges. Rate the level of threat presented by each trigger using the scale below. Finally, list strategies for coping with each trigger that will help you avoid using.

0 ——————— 1 ——————— 2 ——————— 3 ——————— 4 ——————— 5

No Threat   Moderate Threat   Severe Threat

Trigger (external or internal)	Level of threat (0–5)	Coping strategies

Chapter 9   *Managing Thoughts of Using Substances*

Goals

▨   To learn to identify and practice controlling thoughts of using so that you decrease the risk of relapse

▨   To learn to use a variety of coping strategies to manage your thoughts of using

Introduction

Thoughts of using alcohol, tobacco, or other drugs are common. Anyone who stops using a substance will think about it again. It's a normal part of the change process to think about something that you once enjoyed or on which you became dependent. Thoughts of using are often associated with other recovery issues discussed in this workbook, such as cravings, social pressures, family and interpersonal conflicts, and upsetting feelings. A helpful recovery task is to identify and practice controlling thoughts of using so that you decrease the risk of relapse.

Your specific thoughts can contribute to urges or cravings or to feelings such as depression or anger. Changing your thoughts can help you stay sober and feel better about yourself and your life. However, like other recovery skills, controlling thoughts of using takes practice. It also requires you to be aware of when your thoughts are getting control of you and your "addictive thinking" is taking over.

Complete the Managing Thoughts of Using Worksheet found at the end of this chapter. It lists some of the common thoughts experienced by others trying to quit alcohol, tobacco, or other drugs. Note which ones you've had yourself and add your own thoughts. Then write counterstatements to help you practice new ways of thinking.

You can gain greater control over your thoughts of using substances by drawing on a variety of coping strategies:

▦ *Monitor your thoughts.* Completing the Managing Thoughts of Using Worksheet will help you begin the process of monitoring your thoughts of using substances.

▦ *Devise counterstatements.* After you identify some of your specific thoughts, you can develop counterstatements ahead of time to help you fight off your negative thoughts. In the long run, you will have to learn to create counterstatements as new thoughts arise because you cannot prepare for every thought ahead of time.

▦ *Don't act on your thoughts.* Always keep in mind that there is a big difference between thoughts and feelings, and between thoughts and actions. Just because you have a thought doesn't mean you have to act on it. Sometimes all you have to do is ignore your thoughts. Other times, you have to take a more aggressive approach and challenge your thinking.

▦ *Remember the benefits of not using.* Remind yourself of all the benefits you've already experienced from not using, as well as the benefits you expect to experience if you continue not using.

▦ *Remember the problems caused by using.* Remind yourself of the problems actually caused by past use, as well as problems that may occur if you return to substance use.

▦ *Think through the drink or drug.* AA and NA advise you to think through the whole process in a rational way so that you see the potential negative outcome of using as well as the potential positive outcome of not using.

▦ *Practice positive affirmation.* Repeat to yourself statements such as, "I can choose not to use," "I'm capable of staying sober," "I control my thoughts; my thoughts don't control me," or "I want to avoid smoking (drinking or using drugs)." Even if you don't feel comfortable saying or don't believe these affirmations, if you keep repeating them, they may eventually take hold so that you do begin to believe them.

■ *Think of yourself as a sober person.* Start each day with the thought that you are sober from alcohol or other drugs. See yourself as capable of getting through another day without using alcohol, tobacco, or other drugs. View this as a normal part of who you are.

Homework

✎ Complete the Managing Thoughts of Using Worksheet to help you practice new ways of thinking.

Managing Thoughts of Using Worksheet

Instructions: Review the list of common thoughts associated with relapse. Add some personal thoughts to the list. Then, list counterstatements and strategies you can use to change these thoughts in order to control them and prevent them from leading to substance use.

Thoughts	Counterstatements
1. *I'll never use again. I've got my problem under control.*	
2. *A few cigarettes (drinks, lines of cocaine, etc.) won't hurt.*	
3. *I can't have fun or excitement if I don't use.*	
4. *I need something to take the edge off and help me relax.*	
5. *Life is difficult. I need to escape for awhile.*	

Thoughts	Counterstatements
6. I can't fit in with others if they use and I don't.	
7. What's the point in staying sober? It really doesn't matter.	
8. I'm going to test myself to see if I can have just one.	
9. How can I go out with John if I don't drink?	
10. I'll never get out of debt, I might as well get drunk.	
11. I could drink and no one would ever know.	

Chapter 10   *Managing Emotions*

Goals

- To learn how upsetting emotions can cause difficulty in your recovery

- To learn the most common upsetting emotional states and practical strategies for coping with them

Impact of Emotions on Substance Use

Upsetting emotions or feelings are among the most common difficulties in recovery. Feelings such as anger, anxiety, boredom, depression, guilt, and shame can contribute to relapse and cause you unhappiness. Mismanaged feelings can cause problems in your relationships and ability to get along with others.

Many people use alcohol or other drugs to cover up their feelings or make them less painful. However, substances can affect your judgment and exaggerate feelings, making them worse than they actually are. For example, the effects of alcohol or drugs can turn mild irritation or anger into passionate hatred or violence. Under the influence of alcohol, you might inappropriately express simple attraction as unremitting love.

In that sections that follow, each of the most common upsetting emotional states is briefly discussed. This chapter concludes with a discussion of practical strategies to manage your emotions. You'll note that there is a lot of overlap among coping strategies, regardless of the specific emotions or feelings with which you are dealing. After you read the rest of this chapter, complete the Emotions Worksheet. Use this worksheet to rate the emotional states you need to address in your recovery. Then use this information to develop your own recovery coping strategies.

Anger

Difficulty handling angry feelings is one of the biggest roadblocks to recovery. The two most common problems with anger are expressing it too freely and inappropriately, often in hostile, aggressive, passive-aggressive, or violent ways; and letting it build up inside, avoiding direct, appropriate expression of it. Both of these extremes contribute to personal unhappiness and strained personal relationships.

If you "let it all hang out" whenever you feel angry without thinking through the consequences, your goal should be to gain greater control over your expression of anger. You need to think before you act. On the other hand, if you suppress your angry feelings and stew on the inside, you need to give yourself permission to express anger appropriately and to learn healthy ways of sharing your anger with others.

Anxiety

Anxious feelings are common in the early stages of recovery, although for some anxiety persists for months. Anxiety and worry are two sides of the same coin: anxiety refers to the physical side and manifests itself in sweaty palms, fast heartbeat, or edginess; worry refers to the mental side and shows an excess concern about an event, situation, or relationship. "Anticipatory" anxiety refers to the fear that something might happen. Worrying about not getting a job before going on a job interview, worrying about being rejected by another person before asking him or her out on a date, and worrying about having a panic attack in public before leaving your house are examples of anticipatory anxiety. Anxiety and worry become serious problems when they lead to serious personal distress or to avoiding people, situations, or events.

If your anxiety and worry persist despite your being sober from alcohol and drugs, cause you personal distress, or interfere with your life, then you may be suffering from a more severe form of anxiety that is a symptom of a psychiatric disorder. You should consult your therapist and be evaluated to determine if you have one or more of the anxiety disorders. If you have a Panic Disorder, Agoraphobia, or Generalized Anxiety Disorder, you can benefit from treatment by a mental health professional. There are many effective psychological and medication treatments to help you manage an anxiety disorder.

Boredom and Emptiness

Living without alcohol or drugs can be boring, especially if substance use and related activities were a big part of your daily life. The "straight" life can seem like a drag at first. You may miss the action of drinking events such as parties; of getting, preparing, or using drugs; or of socializing with others who are drinking or getting high. As recovery progresses, you may become bored with the routine. You may have to relearn how to have fun without alcohol or drugs and redevelop other interests.

When you quit using alcohol or drugs, you may find you are temporarily bored with your job, your relationships, or how your life is going. Before making any major changes, be sure to think through your options very carefully. This type of boredom is different from being bored with your leisure activities or social life. Hasty decisions regarding a job or relationship should be avoided unless they are necessary; as you relearn to enjoy life without using substances, you may find that an option you considered reasonable earlier would have caused long-term problems.

Emptiness refers to feelings of having a void or empty hole in your life since you quit using alcohol or other drugs. Sometimes you don't experience this feeling until you have had several months of sobriety and begin to wonder, "Is this all there is?" You may discover that sobriety is not all that it's cracked up to be and may feel that nothing in your life seems to have much value or meaning for you. Persistent emptiness is often a symptom of chronic depression or borderline personality disorder. Professional treatment—therapy, medications, or both—can help if you have one or both of these disorders.

Depression

Depression is frequently caused by the acute and chronic effects of alcohol or other drugs on the central nervous system. When you stop using, depression can result from physical withdrawal or from the psychological trauma of giving up something that was important in your life. You can also experience depressed feelings when you closely examine your life and discover that your substance use caused you a lot of problems and losses. Although feelings of depression may go away after stopping alcohol or drug use, they can represent a high risk for relapse, especially if they are not recognized and dealt with effectively.

With continued abstinence from alcohol or other drugs, most depressions go away in time. However, if your depression persists despite several weeks or months of total abstinence and is accompanied by problems with your sleep, appetite, concentration, energy, or sexual interest; hopeless feelings about the future; or thoughts of suicide or the devising of a suicide plan, then seek mental health treatment immediately. If your current therapist is not qualified to assess and treat your depression, ask for assistance in finding a mental health professional who is. All types of clinical depression can be effectively treated with therapy, medications, electroshock therapy, or a combination of these.

Guilt and Shame

Guilt refers to feeling at fault or "bad" about your behaviors—what you did or failed to do. For example, Jerry feels guilty about arguing with his wife, using family money for alcohol, cursing and fighting with his brother when drunk, and getting arrested for driving under the influence. Lavette feels guilty about ignoring her parents and not being available for her children.

Shame refers to feeling unworthy or "bad" about yourself—to feeling defective, weak, or less than others because of your substance use problem. This was best expressed by Jack, addicted to heroin and cocaine, who referred to himself as a "no-good piece of shit."

Strategies for Managing Emotions

Although specific strategies are sometimes needed to cope with a particular feeling, there are many common strategies that can be used to deal with upsetting feelings. Following is a summary of these general strategies, with examples of how they can be used to deal with particular feelings.

- *Recognize your emotions or feelings.* Improving your ability to recognize your feelings sets the stage for coping with them. Early recognition helps you catch problems before they build up. For instance, mild anger or depression is easier to deal with than severe anger or depression that has built up over weeks or longer.

Accept your feelings. Accept your feelings as real and for what they are. Don't judge whether a feeling is "right" or "wrong" or "good" or "bad." If you feel something, then it is real to you and you have to deal with it. The important issue isn't what you feel, but how you let your feelings affect you and how you manage them. Feelings may represent accurate or inaccurate perceptions of situations, but the feelings themselves are real and are neither "right" nor "wrong." Your reactions to your feelings can be effective or ineffective in moving you closer toward your goals, whatever these goals may be.

Know the causes of your feelings. When possible, try to figure out what's contributing to a particular emotional state or feeling. This will help you decide on the best coping strategies. For example, if you feel persistent depression because you are in a primary relationship that is unsatisfying, chaotic, or psychologically abusive, recognizing this problem can improve your depression, especially if you make a decision to do something about it.

Challenge your thoughts. If your thinking is contributing to upsetting emotions or feelings, work on changing how you think and the beliefs that underlie your thinking. For example, if you feel extremely anxious about an upcoming job interview and are telling yourself that you won't get the job, challenge your thinking. Tell yourself, "I will do my best on this interview, which will give me a good chance for the job because I'm well qualified." Practice saying these thoughts, out loud if necessary, to build your confidence and comfort level.

Share your feelings with someone you trust. Sometimes it helps to simply put your feelings into words. Telling a trusted friend or family member, "I feel depressed (furious, anxious, worried, lonely)" can help you feel some relief. Sometimes when you share how you feel, the intensity of the feelings decreases. In addition, you frequently gain a new perspective on what you are experiencing. Putting feelings into words also helps reduce the risk of inappropriately acting on them.

■ *Build structure in your life.* This is particularly important in overcoming boredom, which is common in early recovery. Structure can also help reduce depression and anxiety, particularly if you participate in pleasant activities. Setting specific times and days for activities and sticking to that structure can help you keep going if you find that you are losing direction and momentum.

■ *Use physical or creative activities.* Physical exercise and creative activities help reduce tension and stress, lower depression and anxiety, release anger, and improve self-image. Sports or exercise or music, reading, writing, art, or other creative endeavors can help you express your feelings.

■ *Use inner-directed activities.* Meditation or prayer can help you cope with negative feelings. In addition to reducing stress, anxiety, and depression, these activities can help you feel more energetic, positive, and reflective. For example, prayer is often helpful in reducing feelings of guilt and shame.

■ *Set goals for yourself.* Having goals provides you with the incentive to work toward something that is important to you. Goals can keep you busy, give you something to look forward to, reduce depression or boredom, and give you more structure in your life.

■ *Consider medications for persistent and severe anxiety or depression.* If your severe feelings of anxiety or depression persist despite your being alcohol- or drug-free for a month or longer; if they cause you considerable personal distress; or if they interfere with your ability to function, you may have an additional mental heath problem that could improve with medication. Many non-addictive medicines are available to help treat severe mental health problems such as serious and persistent anxiety, depression, or other moods.

Homework

✎ Complete the Emotions Worksheet to identify and rate the emotional states you need to address in your recovery.

✎ Develop your own recovery coping strategies.

Emotions Worksheet

Instructions: For each emotion below, rate the degree of difficulty you have dealing with these feelings without using alcohol or drugs. Then, choose the two emotions that present the most difficulty in your recovery and identify strategies for coping with them.

0	1	2	3	4	5
None	Low		Moderate		Severe

Emotion	Degree of difficulty coping with emotion (0–5)
1. Anxiety and worry	_____
2. Anger	_____
3. Boredom	_____
4. Depression	_____
5. Feeling empty—like nothing matters	_____
6. Guilt	_____
7. Shame	_____
8. Loneliness	_____

Feeling or emotion	Coping strategies

Chapter 11 *Refusing Offers to Use Substances*

Goals

▪ To learn about direct and indirect social pressures that can lead to relapse

▪ To learn how each social pressure affects your thoughts, feelings, and behaviors

▪ To plan and practice how you will cope with social pressures to use substances

Introduction

One of the biggest and most predictable challenges you face in recovery is resisting social pressures to use alcohol, tobacco, or other drugs. This is especially true in the early months of recovery, when you are just getting used to being sober or not smoking and are not used to refusing offers to use.

Giving in to social pressures is the second most common cause of relapse. You will face direct social pressures when others may offer you alcohol, tobacco, or other drugs and try to influence you to use. Some people might even get right in your face and try to make you feel like there's something wrong with you if you don't use with them. This may make you feel uncomfortable or awkward, especially if you want to fit in and be "one of the crowd."

You will also experience indirect social pressures when others around you are using but don't offer you alcohol, tobacco, or other drugs or try to convince you to use. Being at a picnic, family gathering, party, athletic event, or special occasion such as a wedding or holiday celebration, or even just watching a movie, can trigger a desire to use.

You aid your recovery by preparing to manage people, places, events, and work, family, or social situations that create pressure to use alcohol, tobacco, or other drugs. First, identify the direct and indirect social pressures

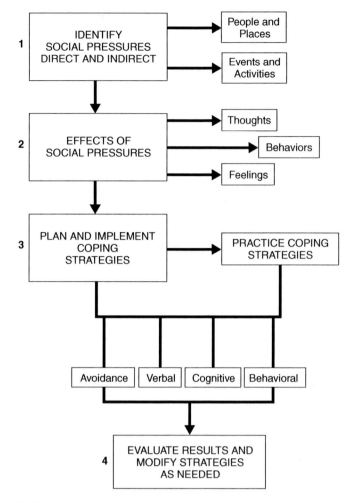

Figure 11.1 Social pressures.

that you are likely to face. Second, be aware of how each direct and indirect social pressure affects your thoughts, feelings, and behaviors. Third, plan and practice how you will cope with social pressures to use substances. Finally, evaluate how you handle each pressure, and change strategies that you think are ineffective or are unlikely to help you resist pressures over time. Figure 11.1 illustrates the issue of social pressures in recovery.

Pressures or offers to use substances come from many sources. People may directly offer you substances, or you may participate in activities in which substances are used. When others are offering you a substance or are using in front of you, a part of you will likely want to use or fit in. Each social pressure influences how you feel, what you think, and ultimately how you act. Anticipating your unique social pressures puts you in a position to develop and practice positive coping strategies.

Although you can avoid many pressures, you cannot avoid them all. Therefore, it helps to plan different strategies you can use to successfully cope with direct and indirect social pressures to use. The key to staying substance-free is having strategies to handle people, places, events, and situations that you are not able to avoid.

Complete the Social Pressures Worksheet to help you identify people, places, and situations that create pressure for you to use substances. After you have identified these pressures, you can develop coping strategies.

Strategies to Resist Offers to Use Substances

Following is a summary of coping strategies to help you identify and resist offers to use substances:

- *Awareness.* Maintain awareness of the direct and indirect social pressures you are likely to face. Pay careful attention to thoughts and feelings generated by various social pressures. Also, be aware of situations in which you are setting yourself up to use. For example, trying to quit alcohol but going to a bar to socialize and trying to quit cocaine or marijuana but attending parties at which others use drugs are examples of "set-up" situations. In set-up situations, your risk of using substances rises considerably.

- *Acceptance.* Keep in mind that a part of you may always be tempted to give in to pressures to use. Learn to accept and live with this aspect of yourself, because it is not likely to go away completely. Usually, the part of you that wants to use is strongest in the first few weeks and months after you stop using.

- *Avoidance.* When possible, avoid high-risk people, places, situations, and events, especially when you feel vulnerable to the influence of others or your own desires to use are strong.

- *Visualization.* Imagine yourself in situations in which others are offering you substances, and visualize yourself continuing to confidently say no. Visualize yourself in control of the situation and continuing to successfully resist internal and external pressures to use.

- *Assertiveness.* Assertiveness refers to clearly and directly stating your intent to not use substances when offered them by others. Assertiveness involves being forthright but not aggressive. You can aid your recovery by practicing saying "no" in a direct and assertive manner before you are actually in situations in which others pressure you to use. Practice with your therapist, with a trusted friend or family member, or alone by looking in the mirror. You can practice assertively refusing offers to use while alone in your car, at home, or at work.

■ *Support group.* Stick with your sober support group. You will learn how others have successfully resisted social pressures to use substances.

■ *Keeping your goals in mind.* Remind yourself privately of your sobriety goals and of the gains you've made so far. Regularly review your short-term goals (next few minutes to next few days) and how they fit in with your long-term goals.

■ *Self-talk.* Give yourself a pep talk about why you want to stay sober and how you are capable of resisting pressures to use. Talk yourself into the desired way of thinking. Don't allow yourself to fall for the thought, "A few won't hurt." Instead, tell yourself, "I don't need to use; I can resist." Do a quick review of the problems your substance use has caused in your life and the benefits of continued sobriety.

■ *Emergency planning.* Some situations can't be avoided, so know your options before a difficult situation occurs. For example, if you feel it is important to attend a social or work event at which alcohol is being served or people are smoking cigarettes, plan to stay only a short time or take with you a supportive friend who knows you are trying to avoid drinking or tobacco use. If you feel the pressure to use mounting in a particular situation, leave immediately. Avoid long discussions about why you don't want to stay or why you aren't drinking or smoking unless you think this will make it easier for you not to use.

Homework

 ✎ Complete the Social Pressures Worksheet.

Social Pressures Worksheet

Instructions: List specific direct or indirect social pressures to use alcohol, tobacco, or other drugs that you expect to face. For each social pressure you list, use the scale below to rate the degree of difficulty you believe you will have coping successfully with that pressure. Finally, list coping strategies you can use to cope with these social pressures.

0 ———————— 1 ———————— 2 ———————— 3 ———————— 4 ———————— 5

No Threat   Moderate Threat   Severe Threat

Social pressures	Degree of difficulty (0–5)	Coping strategies

Chapter 12 *Dealing With Family and Interpersonal Problems*

Goals

▩ To learn to deal with conflicts in your family and interpersonal relationships in order to reduce the risk of relapse

▩ To examine your usual style of relating to others

▩ To begin to formulate and use strategies for resolving your conflicts

Introduction

Problems and conflicts in family and interpersonal relationships are common in recovery and can contribute to relapse if you don't have a plan to deal with them. Conflict, tension, and disagreements are normal parts of human relationships. Not addressing these head-on sets you up to feel angry, frustrated, and unhappy. Therefore, take some time to review the important relationships in your life. See if any of these relationships have serious problems or conflicts, and examine what is causing these problems. Then you can begin to formulate strategies to resolve your interpersonal conflicts.

Sometimes interpersonal problems are very obvious. For example, Art became very angry at his wife for embarrassing and insulting him in front of friends at a dinner party. Helen felt hurt and sad when her husband "forgot" her birthday. Curt and Kathy are constantly arguing over money, sex, the children, and numerous other issues. They have bad feelings toward each other and feel their marriage is on the verge of collapsing.

In contrast, interpersonal conflicts are sometimes subtle, covert, or hidden. In some instances, you may have an idea that something isn't quite right in a relationship. For example, Megan and her sister Jan seldom plan activities with both families, believing that everyone is too busy. On another level, Megan knows deep down that there is an unspoken tension between the two families. Although she has never said this directly to her sister,

Megan does not like or respect Jan's husband and feels uncomfortable being around him. Although Megan is not sure why she's so uncomfortable around her brother-in-law, her discomfort plays a major role in minimizing contact between the two families. In other instances, you may be unaware anything is wrong unless you think long and hard about your relationships with family members. For example, Juan seldom visits his parents, who live within a few hours' drive of his house. Juan and his parents seldom call each other on the phone. The accepted excuse is, "Everyone is very busy these days." However, after further exploration, Juan admitted that he feels angry because every time he visits home, his mother complains nonstop about his father, and his father is hard to be around because he's moody, critical, and not very sociable. It also bothers Juan that his parents seldom make any attempt to visit his family and don't take an interest in the lives of his three children.

Complete the Relationships Worksheet to help you begin to address specific problems you are having with others. Also, complete the Interpersonal Style Worksheet to help you examine your usual style of relating to others. You can use this worksheet to help you determine if there are things you need to change in how you relate to others.

Listening to Experiences of Family Members

It is common for family members to experience hurt or pain as a result of a loved one's substance use problem. Your family is probably no exception. This is especially true if your substance use has led to physical or verbal abuse; unpredictability; irresponsibility in your role as a spouse, parent, or family member; expenditures beyond the family budget; inability to meet the emotional or financial needs of your family; or serious medical problems. Complete the Family Effects Worksheet to help you identify how your family has experienced your substance use problem.

Although it can be painful, it is important to hear from your loved ones what it has been like for them. This requires you to be patient, able to listen without being defensive and making excuses for your behaviors, and willing to accept the emotional pain of family members. Many recovery programs recommend "making amends," a process in which specific steps are taken to reduce the damage caused by a substance use problem (review steps 8 and 9 of AA or NA with a sponsor or counselor). The form that making amends takes can vary from one person to the next. Making your recovery a high priority, involving your family, and listening to their experiences are ways to start the "making amends" process.

Social and Work Relationships

Other relationships can be negatively affected by substance use problems. You may have taken advantage of, lied to, manipulated, ignored, used, or abused your friends or work associates. For example, Serena often had co-workers cover for her and do part of her job when she came in late for work after attending parties the night before. Alex, a college professor, failed to do his share of committee work on a special project for his department, causing other faculty members to feel angry and let down. He often missed meetings, giving a number of poor excuses why he didn't do his share of the work on time.

Ways to Improve Your Relationships

Following are strategies to help you deal with interpersonal problems and conflicts, as well as improve your relationships with family members or other important people in your life:

- *Identify interpersonal conflicts and problems.* Be aware of your specific interpersonal conflicts and problems. Then you can prioritize and work on the one or two that are most important. Remember, these conflicts can be obvious or hidden.

- *Know your role in your conflicts.* Avoid the trap of blaming your problems on others. It usually takes two to have an interpersonal problem. Conflicts in relationships are often caused less by specific events that occur than by your interpretation of these events and your interpersonal style. For example, if you are too aggressive, you need to tone down your aggression. On the other hand, if you are too passive and feel victimized by others, you need to learn to assert yourself more. If your interpersonal style creates serious problems in your relationships, work with your therapist to make changes in how you relate to others.

- *Face your conflicts directly.* Interpersonal conflicts usually don't go away on their own; nothing is accomplished by ignoring them. Deal with your conflicts head-on and avoid the tendency to wish them away or to allow too much time for conflicts to build even more. Maintain control over the expression of your feelings and behaviors when you are discussing conflicts with another person. Accept that conflicts are a normal part of relationships and may provide an opportunity to make relationships better in the long run. There are some couples who seldom express conflict toward each other yet do well in their relationship; it is as if they have an agreement "not to disagree" about anything or enter into critical or conflictual interactions.

- *Express your feelings directly.* Healthy relationships require an ability to share feelings with others. This includes upset feelings such as anger or disappointment as well as positive feelings such as love or appreciation. Many people have an easier time sharing upsetting feelings than positive feelings. However, make sure you express gratitude, love, and other positive feelings toward those closest to you. How you express your feelings is very important. It helps to pay close attention to your tone of voice, facial expressions, body movements, and choice of words. For example, you can tell a loved one in a nonjudgmental and matter-of-fact way that you are angry, implying that you want to communicate and resolve differences; or you can communicate anger in a hostile and negative way that will push the other person away and cause the situation to get worse, not better.

- *Involve your family in recovery and in your life.* When possible, involve your family in some of your treatment sessions and invite them to attend self-help meetings such as Al-Anon or Nar-Anon. There are many advantages to family involvement in your recovery: your family can gain a greater understanding of what it's like for you to stop using substances, provide you with support, and share their feelings and experiences. This sometimes leads to family members becoming involved in a recovery program to deal with their own feelings and issues. If you are heavily involved in mutual support groups, pay close attention to your family too, so that you don't focus all your attention on your recovery and ignore their needs.

■ *Encourage your family to share.* Ask those close to you to share their experiences related to your substance use and behavior so that you gain a greater understanding of their perspective. Be prepared, however, to hear some unpleasant things. Family members and close friends often see the worst side of substance use problems and your behaviors.

■ *Deal with family members or close friends who use illicit drugs.* Avoid being around family members or close friends when they are using illicit drugs. Let them know you are quitting and that it's too difficult to be around them when they use drugs. If your spouse or partner uses drugs, you will face a special stress and will need to figure out how best to deal with it. Whether or not the relationship can continue while you work on your recovery depends on factors such as how long you've been together, how committed you are to each other's welfare, how realistic it is to be in an active relationship and stay drug-free when your partner gets high, and whether your partner is willing to get help or work together so both of you can stay drug-free.

■ *Deal with family members or close friends who smoke or drink.* If you feel too much pressure being around family members or friends who smoke cigarettes or drink alcohol, even if they don't smoke or drink excessively, then you should minimize the time you spend with them when they are smoking or drinking. You can leave such situations entirely if you worry that you might relapse. It also helps to let those who are close to you know that you are trying to quit using alcohol or tobacco. If they visit your house, it is your right not to have alcohol available. It is also your right not to allow anyone to smoke in your house. Letting people know ahead of time makes it easier for them to accept your way of dealing with smokers and drinkers in your house.

■ *Deal directly with your partner if he or she drinks excessively.* If your spouse or partner clearly has an alcohol problem, it will be more difficult to stay sober if he or she drinks in front of you. If your spouse or partner refuses to quit or get help for the drinking problem, then you need to evaluate the relationship to determine if it is too stressful for your recovery. For family members or friends who drink excessively, it is far better to suggest they get help for themselves than to preach about why they should stop drinking.

- *Admit your mistakes.* If you make a mistake in one of your important relationships, don't dwell on it. Instead, admit it to the other person and try to avoid making the same mistake again.

- *Compromise.* Mutual relationships require ability to give and take, or compromise. You must be able to give in at times, even when you feel your position is right. What might be "right" for you individually might not be "right" for the relationship. Compromise also involves doing things with others that you might not particularly enjoy. You do these things because the other person is important to you.

- *Nurture your important relationships.* The best and most satisfying relationships are those that are actively nurtured by positive action. One way of nurturing a relationship is to consciously do and say positive things that the other person will appreciate. In this way, you not only work on problems, but you also work on growth in your relationship.

- *Seek family counseling if problems persist.* If you are unable to resolve specific problems in your family or significant relationships despite trying some of the ideas discussed above or participating in self-help programs, seek family or relationship counseling.

Homework

✎ Complete the Relationships Worksheet.

✎ Complete the Interpersonal Style Worksheet.

✎ Complete the Family Effects Worksheet.

Relationships Worksheet

Instructions: Describe the problematic relationships in your life. Write about what you can do to improve these relationships.

Problem	Ways to improve problem

Interpersonal Style Worksheet

Instructions: Following is a list of statements about interpersonal style. Circle the number that corresponds to the extent to which each statement describes you. Then complete the two items below the list of statements.

	Doesn't describe me		Somewhat describes me			Definitely describes me
1. I say what I think or feel to others and don't hold anything back.	0	1	2	3	4	5
2. I worry about hurting others and hold on to my feelings.	0	1	2	3	4	5
3. I lash out at others when I'm upset or mad at them.	0	1	2	3	4	5
4. I regularly share positive feelings with others.	0	1	2	3	4	5
5. I often criticize others a lot and express negative feelings.	0	1	2	3	4	5
6. I have trouble talking to strangers.	0	1	2	3	4	5
7. I consider myself to be shy and have trouble opening up to others.	0	1	2	3	4	5
8. I relate easily to others and like meeting new people.	0	1	2	3	4	5
9. I let other people close to me know what's important to me.	0	1	2	3	4	5
10. I don't like to argue with others and avoid arguments when I can.	0	1	2	3	4	5
11. I let people take advantage of me too easily.	0	1	2	3	4	5
12. I consider myself to be an aggressive person.	0	1	2	3	4	5
13. I consider myself to be an assertive person.	0	1	2	3	4	5
14. I consider myself to be a pushover and a passive person.	0	1	2	3	4	5
15. I avoid situations where I have to talk in front of other people.	0	1	2	3	4	5
16. I use alcohol, tobacco, or other drugs to help me socialize with others.	0	1	2	3	4	5

Identify one aspect of your interpersonal style that you want to change.

_____

_____

List several steps you can take to help you change this behavior.

_____

_____

_____

_____

_____

_____

Family Effects Worksheet

Instructions: List your family members. Then describe ways in which the behaviors related to your substance use problem have affected each family member.

Family member	Behaviors/consequences of my substance use

Chapter 13   *Building a Recovery Support System*

Goals

- To learn the benefits of having a recovery support system

- To identify people and organizations who can provide you with support

- To work to overcome any barriers to asking for help

- To learn strategies for creating and using an effective recovery support system

Benefits of a Recovery Support System

A *recovery support system* consists of people and organizations that provide you with help and support in your efforts to stop using alcohol, tobacco, or other drugs. A positive support system is associated with a better outcome and has many benefits. It enables you to gain from the strength, hope, experience, and advice of others who care about your recovery. You can lean on others during difficult times as well as share your triumphs and the positive goals that you achieve. You can also share mutual interests or activities with people in your support system.

Many people find it helpful to approach recovery from a "we" instead of an "I" perspective. Although self-reliance is helpful in long-term recovery, in the early stages reliance on others can make a big difference in whether or not you use alcohol or other drugs.

As we discuss in Chapter 14, mutual self-help programs and recovery clubs can play a critical role in your recovery. You can benefit from the fellowship of self-help programs as well as from the specific recovery approach such programs take.

Complete the Recovery Network Worksheet. This worksheet will help you identify people and organizations who can provide you with support. It will also help you see the potential benefits of specific people and organizations.

Barriers to Asking for Help and Support

Although a recovery support network is helpful, you may find it hard to actually ask others for help and support. This may be due to shyness, fear, guilt over your previous behavior, lack of self-confidence, poor social skills, or a belief that you should be able to handle your own problems, that you are not worthy of others' efforts to help you, or that others will reject you if you seek their support. Another barrier is choosing the wrong people to ask for support. These include people who won't understand or accept your interest in staying off alcohol or other drugs, or who believe you must be out of your mind for wanting to stop.

Once you identify barriers that will interfere with your ability to ask others for support, you can then work on overcoming these barriers. For example, Tina identified being shy and being fearful of rejection as her major barriers to asking for help. She worked with her therapist to practice initiating conversations with others. After successfully testing this out over time, Tina then worked on requesting help and support from other members of AA. She dealt with her fear of rejection by examining what evidence she had that others would reject her. In fact, she discovered that there was only a single case of another person's rejecting her, and it so happened that this person was notorious for being antisocial and hard to get along with. Tyrone identified pride and excessive self-reliance as his barriers to asking for help. A star athlete who always played a major role on the team, he was not used to being in a position of asking for help from others. When he came to believe that his self-reliance wouldn't be threatened by reaching out for help, he took the risk. Tyrone feels the risk paid off because he was able to benefit from the experiences of another athlete who had overcome a drug problem. This connection helped Tyrone stay focused on his academic and athletic goals and deal more effectively with his drug abuse.

How to Ask for Help and Support

When you choose the right people, there's a very good chance they will respond favorably to your request for help and support. Ask for what you want directly and specifically. Consider the following examples:

"Frank, I'm interested in your being my sponsor. I really like what you've done with your recovery and your straightforward approach to telling it like it is."

"Marie, I quit smoking cigarettes and I'm asking that when you come to my house for dinner next weekend, if you feel like smoking, please do it outside on the porch. Even smelling smoke makes me want to light up, so I appreciate your understanding of this request."

"Dad, I finally accepted that my drinking was a serious problem, so I'm on the wagon. I won't be serving any liquor at Tim's graduation party and hope you are OK with this."

"Lynn, I'd like to go with you to some NA meetings. I'm nervous about going by myself and would enjoy your company."

"David, I really enjoyed it when we worked out in the past. I'm changing some bad habits and going back to the gym. I wouldn't mind running and working out with you."

"Melissa, I know you kicked cigarettes a couple years ago. I can't take my work breaks with the others who smoke now. Do you mind if I join you sometime during break time so my temptation to smoke isn't so bad?"

"Fran, I want to get high so bad I can almost feel the drugs going into my veins. Instead of copping drugs, I stopped at a gas station and I'm calling you before I pick up like you suggested. Can we meet after the NA meeting for a cup of coffee and to talk?"

Ways to Develop a Support Network

Following is a summary of strategies to help you develop and effectively use a recovery support system:

- *Identify supportive people.* Know who you want to be involved in your network. Consider how they can help and how and when you can ask them.

- *Ask for help directly.* When you make a request for help and support, be as specific as you can. Face your reluctance to ask for help and take a risk. Practice ahead of time what you will say if you think this will make you more comfortable and more likely to follow through with making a specific request. Also, if you choose people who were upset and hurt by your substance use problem, be sure to make amends first (see Chapter 12) to reduce some of the bad feelings that may still exist.

■ *Get involved in organizations.* In addition to self-help organizations specifically related to recovery, think about church, community, social, or athletic organizations. Being active in organizations can increase your sense of connection to others and provide you opportunities to learn from others and participate in leisure, athletic, political, creative, or religious activities.

■ *Be active.* If you are in a recovery organization, make a point of talking to someone else in the program at least once a day, especially in the early weeks and months of recovery. Keep at list of at least 10 names and phone numbers of others in recovery.

■ *Face your excuses for resisting help.* Everyone has reasons why he or she cannot ask for help and support, even if he or she believes it could be helpful ("Yeah, but…"). Figure out what your excuses are. Consider the following examples:

"I know the others who are trying to quit smoking like me will be glad to talk to me, but I don't want to bother them."

"I know getting a sponsor can help me stay off cocaine, but what if I pick someone who isn't working a good program?"

"I know I should tell my parents I don't want to be around them when they are drinking, but I don't want to hurt their feelings."

■ *Focus on pleasant activities, not just recovery issues.* If you belong to a recovery program, find out about enjoyable social events and activities that the program sponsors or that other members participate in. Do something fun at least once a week.

Homework

✍ Complete the Recovery Network Worksheet.

Recovery Network Worksheet

Instructions: Identify people and organizations that you believe can be a vital part of your recovery network. Then, list the potential benefits of having these individuals and organizations as part of your recovery.

People/organizations	Potential benefits

Chapter 14   *Self-Help Programs and Recovery Clubs*

Goals

- To learn about the different types of mutual self-help programs available

- To determine which type of program may work for you

Introduction

Numerous self-help programs exist to help you cope with your substance use problem. The most common of these are Alcoholics Anonymous (AA) and Narcotics Anonymous (NA). All self-help programs involve people with alcohol or drug problems helping each other out. Whereas some people maintain lifelong involvement in self-help programs, others use them for a limited period of time. Some people go in and out, using self-help programs whenever they feel the need. After reading this chapter, complete the Self-Help Program Worksheet to help you determine potential benefits of a self-help program. A list of self-help organizations, including addresses and phone numbers, is included in the Appendix.

Although self-help programs vary in their philosophies and approaches, most involve the following elements:

- *Fellowship.* This involves people with similar problems helping each other deal with their alcohol problems, drug problems, or both. They do this by sharing experiences in and out of meetings, "sponsoring" newcomers (commonly done in AA and NA), and being available to talk about recovery issues of mutual concern, such as how to deal with cravings to use, how to recover from a lapse or relapse, or how to undo the damage inflicted on family members or other people as a result of substance use.

- *Recovery meetings.* These involve discussing recovery issues or listening to personal stories of others who share their experiences with substance use and recovery.

- *Program steps or guidelines.* These involve particular steps you can take to deal with your alcohol or drug problem. Programs such as the 12 steps of AA and NA are seen by many as a way of life, not just a way of overcoming a substance use problem.

- *Self-help literature.* Many booklets, books, and tapes are available to provide you with information, inspiration, or hope. Many are written by people in recovery from an alcohol or drug problem.

- *Social events.* Some self-help programs such as AA or NA sponsor social events such as holiday celebrations or activities. These events provide an alcohol- and drug-free environment in which you can have fun, meet other people, and not feel pressured to use substances.

12-Step Self-Help Programs

Alcoholics Anonymous and Narcotics Anonymous

AA, NA, and other 12-step recovery programs are available at no cost to any person who wants to stop drinking or using other drugs. These self-help programs are based on the premise that members can help each other recover from substance use problems. These are the largest and most accessible of all the self-help programs, with meetings held throughout the world.

AA and NA view alcoholism and drug addiction as diseases that have physical, psychological, social, and spiritual components. Recovery is a process that addresses these different domains in the 12 steps of recovery, in the other aspects of AA and NA such as discussion or lead meetings, or between "sponsor" and "recovering member." Members help each other by exchanging phone numbers, attending meetings together, providing support to one another, and celebrating positive accomplishments in recovery.

Within AA and NA there are a variety of "specialty" meetings. These include meetings for specific groups of recovering individuals such as those new to recovery, gays or lesbians, businessmen, young people, healthcare professionals, and those with dual disorders (substance use problems and psychiatric illness).

A major component of 12-step programs is reliance on a higher power for help. Although many people find this acceptable and helpful in their recovery, others are uncomfortable with anything related to spirituality or religion. You have several options if this part of the program makes you uncomfortable: use only the aspects of the 12-step programs that you are comfortable with philosophically; find other self-help programs such as Rational Recovery (RR) or Self-Management and Recovery Training (SMART) that don't emphasize the need for a higher power (see Appendix for information); or approach the issue of a higher power with an open mind to see if any aspect of this recovery component can help you.

Smokers Anonymous and Nicotine Anonymous

These programs adapt the 12 steps for smokers. Similar to all 12-step programs, these focus on not only stopping the behavior (i.e., smoking), but also on making changes in yourself and your lifestyle to help you stay off cigarettes or nicotine.

Dual Recovery Anonymous

This program is similar to AA and NA with the main exception that its members are recovering from dual problems of substance use and psychiatric disorders. The 12 steps have been modified to accommodate the psychiatric illness.

Other 12-Step Programs

Numerous other 12-step programs exist for drug addiction and other life problems. These include Emotions Anonymous, Emotional Health Anonymous, Gamblers Anonymous, Marijuana Anonymous, Overeaters Anonymous, Sex Addictions Anonymous, Spenders Anonymous, and Sex and Love Addicts Anonymous.

Other Self-Help Programs

There are other self-help programs as alternatives to AA and NA. Each program has a specific philosophy, approach to recovery, meeting format, and written literature. The more common of these programs include Rational Recovery, SMART Recovery, Women for Sobriety, Men for Sobriety, and Moderation Management. Most of these self-help programs attempt to help people quit substances and stay alcohol- or drug-free. The exception is Moderation Management, a controversial program developed for individuals who don't have a physical dependence on alcohol. Moderation Management is also not recommended for anyone who has serious physical or psychiatric problems caused or worsened by alcohol use, or for anyone taking medications that interact with alcohol. Moderation Management is not a "controlled drinking" program and is intended for problem drinkers, not chronic drinkers. Moderation Management has a nine-step program of recovery that aims to help the person moderate his or her alcohol use.

The main problem with these alternative self-help programs is that there are a limited number of meetings available and no meetings at all in some areas. Also, some treatment programs and professionals recommend mainly the 12-step programs of AA or NA.

Recovery Clubs and Clubhouses

Some areas have recovery clubs or clubhouses for people in recovery from alcohol or other drug problems. These organizations provide an alcohol- and drug-free atmosphere in which you can attend recovery meetings or dances or other social events. Many offer the chance to informally chat with others over a cup of coffee or a meal.

Using Self-Help Resources

You can help yourself in several ways regarding self-help programs and recovery clubs or clubhouses:

- *Become educated.* Become informed about various self-help programs and recovery clubs or clubhouses available in your area.

Read informational pamphlets or books such as *Alcoholics Anonymous* (the "Big Book"), *Narcotics Anonymous* (the "Basic Text"), *The Small Book* (Rational Recovery), and *Moderate Drinking* (Moderation Management) to learn about the various programs (see the Suggested Additional Readings). These materials can be purchased in bookstores, through the organization that sponsors the self-help program, or at local self-help meetings.

▪ *Consider your options.* Once you have found out what self-help programs are available in your area, consider the pros and cons of each program that appeals to you. You don't have to agree with a particular self-help program's philosophy to gain something from it. Don't ask yourself, "Will I like it?" but rather, "Can it help me?"

▪ *Keep an open attitude.* Many people have unrealistic ideas about how self-help programs work or what goes on in them. For example, some believe they have to stand in front of a crowd of strangers and confess they are an alcoholic or a drug addict. You don't usually have to talk unless you want to. For the most success, consider how a particular program can help you instead of thinking about what you don't like about it.

▪ *Consider previous experiences.* Review your previous involvement in self-help programs or recovery clubs or clubhouses to figure out what was most helpful and unhelpful. Even if a particular program wasn't helpful in the past, that doesn't mean it cannot be of benefit now. On the other hand, if you've really tried to use a particular program only to find you didn't benefit from it, then try another type of self-help program.

▪ *Try several meetings.* Attend up to a dozen different meetings before you make a final decision as to whether or not a self-help program can help you. It's hard to judge by just a few meetings, because meetings can vary in content and in how they are conducted. You may feel more open-minded at some meetings than at others.

▪ *Get a meeting list and names of contacts.* Ask your therapist for a list of meetings in your area or consult the phone book for the phone numbers of the self-help organizations in which you are interested. If you are extremely uncomfortable going to meetings by yourself, ask your therapist for names of people who might go with you, ask another person in recovery to go with you, or call the local office or the self-help organization and ask for a temporary sponsor.

- *Develop contacts.* Get a list of telephone numbers of other self-help group members and learn to reach out for help and support. If you have trouble asking for support from others, ask your therapist to help you learn ways of asking for help.

- *Find something beneficial.* Rather than focusing on what you don't like about a particular program or meeting, find something positive, no matter how small. It is your responsibility to find something from the program or meeting that will be of help to you.

- *Establish a support group.* Find a group of people you like and feel a connection with, regardless of the group philosophy. The connections with others who have similar problems can be as beneficial as or even more beneficial than the group philosophy.

Homework

 ✎ Complete Self-Help Program Worksheet.

Self-Help Program Worksheet

Instructions: Complete the following items to help you decide how self-help programs could help you stop using alcohol, tobacco, or other drugs and help reduce the chances or relapse.

1. Describe what it is like for you to ask others for help and support.

   _____

   _____

   _____

   _____

2. Summarize your previous experiences in self-help programs (pro and con).

   _____

   _____

   _____

   _____

3. List potential drawbacks of participating in self-help programs.

   _____

   _____

   _____

   _____

4. List potential benefits of participating in self-help programs.

   _____

   _____

   _____

   _____

5. Which specific self-help program(s) do you think would benefit you in quitting or staying off alcohol, tobacco, or other drugs?

   _____

   _____

   _____

   _____

Chapter 15   *Medications for Substance Use Problems*

Goals

- ▓ To learn about the various types of medication that can help you recover.

- ▓ To understand the reasons why some people may have problems with medication

- ▓ To learn about withdrawal symptoms

- ▓ To understand the effects of drug and alcohol use on psychiatric medications

- ▓ To determine whether or not you need medication

Medications for Addiction

Medications can help you safely and comfortably withdraw from substances such as alcohol, opiates, or sedatives if you have a physical addiction. The medicines used will depend on the drug or drugs on which you are dependent.

Medicines may be used to "replace" the addictive drug. Methadone maintenance (MM), for example, helps heroin addicts transfer their addiction from street drugs to methadone, which can be administered and monitored in a licensed narcotic addiction clinic. Nicotine replacement therapy in the form of gum (Nicorette), patches (NicoDerm), or nasal spray (Nicotrol) helps many people stop smoking.

Antagonist or mixed replacement (agonist/antagonist) medications are used for some opiate addicts. Naltrexone (ReVia) "antagonizes" the effects of heroin so the addict does not get high if he ingests heroin while using it. Buprenorphine (Buprenex), a newer medication, has both replacement and antagonist effects. It can be used to help the addicted person withdraw from heroin or other opiate drugs. Buprenorphine also helps the addict in maintenance therapy. This drug is administered at licensed narcotic addiction clinics or by private physicians who have special training and certification to use it in their office-based practices.

Medications may be used to reduce craving among alcoholics and those addicted to smoking. Naltrexone (ReVia) and acamprosate (Campral) reduce the alcoholic's craving and bupropion (Zyban) reduces the smoker's craving.

Disulfiram (Antabuse) serves as "aversive therapy" for alcoholics. If the alcoholic drinks with disulfiram in her system (it stays in the system for up to 7 to 14 days after her last dose), she becomes sick. This aversive reaction is a motivator for some alcoholics not to drink. The idea is to "buy time" so that the person does not drink when craving alcohol. If she waits to drink alcohol until disulfiram is out of her system, there is a good chance that her craving to drink will be gone.

One of the problems you may face is the pressure from others in recovery not to use any drugs. Some misguided people have the wrong attitude about "medications" and perceive these as the same as "addictive" substances, and hence do not see their potential benefits. This is especially true of methadone, a medication that has helped many people remain drug-free while improving their lives. Remember, others are entitled to their opinion, but you have the right to use medications to help you in your recovery from an addiction to alcohol or other drugs.

Attitudes About Taking Medication

There are several attitude problems you may face regarding medication. First, you have to accept that medications for addiction or a psychiatric illness are different than alcohol or drugs used to get high. You are taking medications to treat a disorder and get better. You should not feel guilty for taking medication or believe that they are a "crutch" or you are "weak" for needing them. Some people resent the idea that they have to take a medicine for an addiction or a psychiatric disorder. They argue with doctors, therapists, and family members. Some even refuse medicine altogether or take it for only a short time and then stop.

A second problem is wanting to stop taking medication once your symptoms are under control and you feel better. Never stop your medications unless you first talk this over with your therapist and doctor. Many people relapse to addiction or psychiatric illness after they stop or cut down on their medication following a period in which they feel better. Just as you shouldn't stop taking medications for high blood pressure, diabetes, or other medical conditions on your own, you should not stop taking medications for an addiction or psychiatric disorder without first talking to the people taking care of you. Any desire to stop on your own should first be discussed with your doctor, therapist or counselor, or AA/NA sponsor if you have one. Another person can help you examine your "real" reasons for wanting to stop taking medications.

A third problem is side effects from medication. If you are having unpleasant side effects that don't go away, call your doctor to ask if your medicines need to be changed or you need to do something to offset these side effects. Some side effects go away in time. Others become more tolerable over time.

A fourth problem is feeling frustrated that your symptoms are not improving as much as you would like. Some individuals do not respond to certain medications as well as others. They may try several different types of medication over a period of time and feel very frustrated if they don't quickly find the medication that works for them. You have to be patient if this happens. We have observed that many people addicted to opiate drugs who undergo detoxification become very impatient when their symptoms do not improve as quickly as they would like. They sometimes make poor decisions and leave a detox program against medical advice as a result. Medications aren't equally effective with everyone who has the same symptoms.

A fifth problem is expecting medications to make all of your symptoms or problems go away. While medication can control or reduce symptoms, some chronic or persistent symptoms may remain with you. You have to learn to live with these as best you can. Also, medications cannot take away problems in your life. That is why medications should be used with therapy and/or participation in self-help programs such as AA or NA.

Withdrawing from Addictive Drugs

As we discussed in Chapter 4, if you have a physical addiction to alcohol or other drugs and have been unable to quit on your own, or if you have a history of complications related to withdrawal, such as seizures, DTs, severe depression, psychotic symptoms, or suicidal feelings, you should seek medical treatment to help you through the withdrawal process. Medications can reduce, stop, or prevent withdrawal symptoms. Professionals who help you through the withdrawal process can also help you find the type of treatment you need for ongoing help with your addiction, since detox in and of itself has little value if not followed by other treatment.

Alcohol Withdrawal

Withdrawal symptoms usually start on the first day and peak on the second or third day after a person completely stops or significantly cuts down alcohol use after drinking heavily for several days or longer. Symptoms include tremors of the hands, tongue, and eyelids; nausea and vomiting; weakness; sweating; elevated blood pressure or tachycardia; anxiety; depression or irritability; and low blood pressure when in an upright position. More severe cases of withdrawal may include delusions (false beliefs), hallucinations, seizures, or agitated behavior. Alcohol withdrawal can last several days and may involve taking depressant medications such as Valium, Librium, or Serax.

Depressant Withdrawal

Heavy or prolonged use of other depressant drugs such as sedatives and tranquilizers can cause withdrawal symptoms similar to alcohol withdrawal symptoms. Withdrawal from depressant drugs is done by gradually tapering off the drug the person is addicted to, or by substituting a drug that is similar in its action on the central nervous system. Withdrawal from some of the longer-acting tranquilizers takes more than a few days.

Opiate or Narcotic Withdrawal

Symptoms of withdrawal from heavy, prolonged use of opiates or narcotics include runny nose, tearing eyes, dilated pupils, gooseflesh, sweating, diarrhea, yawning, mild hypertension, tachycardia, fever, and insomnia. Symptoms start 6 to 12 hours after the last drug dose, peak on the second or third day, and usually end within 7 to 14 days, depending on the specific drugs used and the length of the addiction. Medically supervised withdrawal from opiates or narcotics involves taking methadone, buprenorphine, or clonidine.

Cocaine and Stimulant Withdrawal

Depressed mood, fatigue, disturbed sleep, and increased dreaming are symptoms that sometimes occur during withdrawal from heavy, prolonged use of stimulant drugs. Although there are no severe physical withdrawal symptoms associated with addiction to cocaine or stimulant drugs, medications may be used to help someone through the withdrawal process.

Many medications have been studied in the treatment of cocaine and other stimulant addiction. While there is some benefit to these medications, none has been consistently helpful. These medications include agonists that mimic cocaine effects (e.g., amphetamine, methylphenidate, and pemoline), cocaine antagonists that block cocaine effects (e.g., bupropion and mazindol), and medications that decrease cocaine reinforcements (e.g., SSRI antidepressants, baclofen, and gabapentin).

Nicotine Withdrawal

Symptoms of nicotine withdrawal usually begin within hours of stopping or significantly reducing tobacco use after heavy, regular use. These symptoms include tobacco cravings, irritability, anxiety, concentration problems, restlessness, headaches, drowsiness, and gastrointestinal disturbances. Nicotine gum or patches can be used to help someone gradually withdraw from use of tobacco products such as cigarettes. Nicotine gums or patches allow nicotine-dependent people to gradually wean themselves from tobacco. Nicotine gum helps to minimize nicotine withdrawal symptoms and to decrease the person's risk of relapse in the early weeks and months of being tobacco-free. However, it can be addictive, and you should not use it if you have medical conditions such as a recent myocardial infarction, vasospastic disease, cardiac arrhythmia, esophagitis, peptic ulcers, or inflammation of the mouth or throat. Some people complain of side effects such as hiccups, nausea, jaw irritation, and bad taste. A nicotine patch can help stop withdrawal symptoms by decreasing tension, anxiety, irritability, restlessness, and nicotine cravings. The patch gradually releases nicotine into the system, usually over a period of 24 hours. Patches can be used up to several weeks or longer to help a person withdraw from nicotine.

Nicotine nasal sprays and nicotine inhalers are two other approaches to decreasing people's urge to smoke.

Case Example: Lorraine (Nicotine Patch)

Lorraine is a 59-year-old teacher with a 35-year history of dependence on cigarettes. She had quit smoking on her own many times but always relapsed within several weeks. Lorraine was smoking nearly three packs a day when she decided to try a nicotine patch rather than quit "cold turkey." Over the course of a month, Lorraine was able to stop cigarettes completely and has been smoke-free for 9 months. She reports occasional cravings but feels she's able to talk herself out of wanting to smoke. Lorraine also exercises regularly and has learned some ways of reducing stress in her life to decrease the likelihood of smoking to cope with stress.

Maintaining Abstinence From Addictive Drugs

Abstinence From Alcohol

Disulfiram, known by the trade name Antabuse, is a drug used by some people to help "buy time" when they want to drink. Antabuse will stay in your system for a week or longer, so if you decide to drink, you have to wait for Antabuse to clear your system to avoid getting sick. If you ingest any alcohol while Antabuse is in your system, you will get sick because Antabuse interrupts the body's normal process of metabolizing alcohol. The idea behind this drug is simple: it is supposed to deter you from using any alcohol, but if you do drink and get sick, the punishment will deter you from drinking in the future. Antabuse usually is recommended only for the short term (6 months or less) due to its effects on the liver. Also, a fatal reaction between alcohol and Antabuse can occur, so it is not recommended if you tend to act impulsively.

Naltrexone was initially developed for use with opiate addicts to block the euphoric effects of these drugs. More recently, it has been used with alcoholics. Known by the trade name ReVia, naltrexone appears to block the effects of the body's own opioids, which reduces the reinforcing properties of alcohol and thus the desire to drink. You cannot use ReVia if you are currently using any narcotic drugs or have hepatitis or liver disease.

A newer medication used in Europe and recently used in the United States is acamprosate (trade name Campral). Results from multiple studies show that this medication increases the number of alcohol-dependent individuals who maintain abstinence from alcohol after they become sober. It appears to lessen the craving to drink alcohol.

Case Example: Christina (Naltrexone)

■ *Christina is a 38-year-old with a very long history of alcohol dependence. Although she had been in numerous treatment programs and had participated in AA meetings, the longest she had ever been sober was 5 weeks. Christina returned to outpatient treatment as a result of a DWI charge. Given her strong cravings for alcohol and inability to stay sober with other treatments, Christina agreed to use naltrexone and attend therapy sessions twice per week. She has now been sober for over 7 months and strongly believes that ReVia (naltrexone) has helped her recover. Christina has also been able to decrease the frequency of her therapy sessions.* ■

Abstinence From Opiates

Drugs such as Trexan or LAAM are opiate antagonists that block the euphoric effects of heroin or other opiate drugs. Blocking the euphoric effects of opiates will reduce your desire to continue using these drugs, thus reducing your risk of relapse.

Some people who become dependent on heroin or other opiate drugs have an extremely difficult time staying drug-free, even though they have participated in rehabilitation or other treatment programs. Methadone maintenance (MM) is a treatment in which use of the opiate drug is stopped and methadone, a longer-acting opiate, is substituted. MM works best in combination with counseling or therapy. Regular doses of methadone will help you avoid using opiate drugs. Very importantly, MM, when combined with counseling, will enable you to resume normal life activities such as work. Although it is intended as an interim treatment of a few months to a year or two, some people end up using MM for many years. Methadone can be given only at specially licensed clinics.

Case Example: Patrick (Methadone Maintenance)

Patrick is a 34-year-old nurse whose addiction to heroin has caused him to lose a marriage, get fired from one job, and experience numerous other legal, emotional, and financial problems. Although he had been detoxified and had participated in several rehabilitation programs, outpatient therapy, and NA, he was unable to stay drug-free for longer than a few months until he got in a methadone maintenance program. Patrick has not used heroin or any other drugs or alcohol in almost 2 years. He has been able to return to gainful employment and feels his life is much improved. Talking about daily hassles and stresses with his MM counselor helps Patrick keep from using alcohol or other drugs.

Abstinence From Cocaine

Drugs such as bromocriptine or amantadine are sometimes used to reduce a person's craving for cocaine. Results of studies on their effectiveness are mixed, and they are not used in many treatment programs.

Medications for Coexisting Psychiatric Disorder

If you suffer from a psychiatric disorder in addition to your substance use problem, you may benefit from the use of medications. Psychiatric medications such as antidepressants sometimes have the added benefit of reducing desires to use substances such as alcohol. You should be aware that some psychiatric medications such as tranquilizers and sedatives can be addictive and lead to relapse to substance use.

Sometimes, well-meaning counselors or members of 12-step groups take an "all or none" view of medications and take the position that any medication used to change moods is not necessary. Remember, anyone can offer you an opinion, but only a qualified physician, psychologist, or mental health professional is in the position to know whether or not medications may be helpful for a particular psychiatric condition.

Effects of Drug and Alcohol Use on Psychiatric Medications

Using alcohol, street drugs, or other nonprescribed medications can have a negative effect on antidepressant medications by causing the level of medication in your blood to increase or decrease. You can get a false reading of the level of medication in your blood in some cases because alcohol or other drug use can actually temporarily cover up symptoms by increasing your blood level of medication. Even small amounts of alcohol or other drugs can have a negative effect on medications. In some instances, mixing medication with alcohol or drugs can cause serious complications with psychiatric symptoms.

Substance use can also lower your motivation to comply with psychiatric medications. Many people complain that their medication does not work, yet they continue using alcohol and drugs. If you continue to drink or use drugs, do not expect to get the maximum benefit from medications. Also, be aware that some doctors may not prescribe psychiatric medications unless you agree to abstain from substances.

Case Example: BJ (Mood Stabilizer)

BJ is a 46-year-old laborer with a long history of abuse of and dependence on alcohol, marijuana, and crack cocaine. His addiction has led to many problems and has played a major role in a long string of fights with other men. However, even in the absence of substance use, BJ is a violent man. After being sober for almost 2 months, he continued to experience severe mood swings with intense anger and irritability. These mood swings had always led him back to alcohol or drug use in the past. BJ was diagnosed with a mood disorder and reluctantly agreed to take Depakote, a mood stabilizer. To his surprise, he felt much better and did not impulsively return to drug use as he had in the past. For the first time in his life, BJ has been sober from both alcohol and drugs for over a year. He also reports that he hasn't been in any fights since starting the medication, and he feels his irritability and bad temper are now under control.

Medications as Adjunctive versus Primary Treatments

For ongoing recovery from alcohol or other drug problems, you should use medications in conjunction with therapy, counseling, or participation in self-help programs. The amount of time you would take medications depends on your particular history of substance use, problems caused by your use, and your response to prior treatment.

How to Know If You Need Medication

You should discuss any questions about medications with a therapist or physician who is knowledgeable about recovery from substance use problems. Medications can help your ongoing recovery if:

■ You have been unable to stay off alcohol, tobacco, or other drugs for longer than a few months at a time.

■ You have tried other forms of treatment and still gone back to using alcohol, tobacco, or other drugs.

■ You feel it is very difficult not to drink or use tobacco or other drugs, although you know you should quit and want to quit.

■ You often feel overwhelmed by cravings and strong desires to use alcohol, tobacco, or other drugs.

■ You have a lot to lose if you relapse, such as an important relationship, a job, or your professional status or license.

■ Your physical health or mental stability has been greatly affected by your substance use and will continue to get worse if you use.

■ You believe medications will help you benefit more from other forms of treatment such as professional therapy or participation in self-help groups.

Sometimes, questions are raised about the risks and side effects of medications. You should discuss these questions with a physician and with your therapist so you can do a cost/benefit analysis (Table 15.1). Usually, the risks and costs of taking medications are small in comparison with the risks of continued abuse of or dependency on alcohol, tobacco, or other drugs.

Table 15.1 Questions to Ask Your Doctor About Medications

1. What is the purpose of this medication?
2. When should I take this medicine, should it be taken with food, or should I avoid eating right before or after taking it?
3. How long will it take for medications to have an effect on my symptoms, and which symptoms are most likely to be relieved?
4. How will I know this medication isn't working for me?
5. What are the side effects, will they go away, and if they don't go away, what can I do about these, and which should I report immediately to my doctor?
6. What are the risks of not taking this medication?
7. How long will I need to take medication?
8. What happens if I drink alcohol or use other drugs while I'm taking this medication?
9. Are there other medicines, including over-the-counter drugs, that interact with this medication?
10. What are the dangers of missing dosages of medications or taking more than prescribed?
11. If I feel like quitting my medications, what should I do before stopping?

Medication Seeking

Some people look for a "magic" medication that will cure their psychiatric illness or addiction and make everything better for them. They think that anytime their symptoms worsen or new ones develop, some pill will magically take these symptoms away, or they hope that a medication can make them feel better when they have serious problems at work or in their relationships. Regardless of your symptoms or how you respond to medication, you have to learn coping skills to change your life and manage your disorders. While medications are very helpful for many types of addiction or psychiatric disorders and a major form of treatment for some, other strategies are also needed, which is why counseling or therapy can be very helpful.

Coping With People Who Pressure You to Stop Taking Medication

Since other people may suggest that you stop taking your medications, it helps to think ahead and plan how to handle this situation if it arises. You should think about this the same way that you think about heart medication. If another person told you to get off your heart medication, would you stop it? Of course not! The same holds true for medication used for an addiction and/or a psychiatric illness. Tell people straight out that you need the medication, question why they would want you to stop a medication used to treat a serious disorder, or tell them that you don't appreciate their poor advice.

Some people believe they have to "white knuckle" it, that no matter how severe their symptoms are, they should cope with them without medication. We have seen people suffer needlessly because they felt that they should not take medication. The reality is that some people cannot recover from an addiction or psychiatric disorder unless they are on medications. Remind yourself what can happen if you stop taking medication and the benefits you have experienced. Ask your sponsor or treatment team for other ideas or ways to cope with pressures from others to stop taking your medications. Ask other men and women in your program how they dealt with this pressure.

Relapse Prevention, Progress Measurement, and Co-occurring Psychiatric Disorders

Chapter 16 *Relapse Prevention: Reducing the Risk of Relapse*

Goals

- ▓ To understand the difference between a lapse and relapse

- ▓ To learn about relapse prevention

- ▓ To learn to identify and manage relapse warning signs and high-risk factors

Lapse and Relapse

A *lapse* refers to an initial episode of substance use following a period of abstinence. A lapse may or may not lead to more substance use. You always run the risk that a lapse will turn into a *relapse*, in which you continue to use alcohol or other drugs.

A lapse or relapse is the last link in a chain of decisions. Before you actually pick up that first drink, cigarette, or other drug, you will make decisions that are "set-ups" for relapse. For example, going to a bar to drink soda 2 weeks after quitting alcohol is a relapse set-up. Hanging out with friends who snort cocaine or smoke marijuana and trying to abstain while they get high is a relapse set-up. This is why it's important to be aware of the seemingly irrelevant decisions that you usually make before your relapse. For example, Rick had abstained from alcohol for over 7 months when he met someone at a bar to discuss a potential job. Although he had no intention of drinking when this arrangement was made, once he was in the bar, Rick found it impossible to resist his desires to drink. Lisa, off cigarettes for 6 weeks, was waiting for a table in a restaurant when the hostess told her one was available in the smoking section. Lisa didn't think it would be a problem to take the table. However, smelling others' cigarette smoke triggered Lisa to buy a pack of cigarettes on the way home. Both Rick and Lisa made decisions that seemed to have nothing to do with their subsequent use of alcohol and tobacco. However, these decisions set them up for relapse.

Response to a Lapse or Relapse

How you respond to an initial lapse has a big impact on whether or not you have a full-blown relapse. If you scold yourself, see yourself as a failure, and give yourself negative messages such as, "I'm not capable of stopping" or "I just can't control myself," you are likely to continue using. On the other hand, if you view your lapse as a mistake and an opportunity to strengthen your resolve, it can be a good learning experience. Even if you end up having a full-blown relapse, you can learn much by reviewing what led up to it and why, where, and how it happened.

Relapse Prevention

Relapse prevention (RP) refers to all the strategies and skills that you use to avoid substance use, modify your lifestyle, and reduce stress so that you lower your risk of relapse. Effective RP requires you to be motivated to change and to develop confidence in your ability to handle stressful situations.

RP involves thinking ahead and anticipating the problems or stresses that could lead you back to alcohol, tobacco, or other drug use. By identifying these potential problems (also referred to as "high-risk" situations) ahead of time, you can plan ways of coping with the problems without substance use. It's much better to have a plan for coping with a relapse and not need it than to need a plan and not have one. This is similar to the rationale for a fire drill: it's better to know what to do in case of a fire than to be caught off guard. RP prepares you ahead of time for what could happen.

Relapse Management

Relapse management prepares you to handle actual lapses or relapses so that you can minimize the damage. You have to learn to act quickly and catch your mistakes before the situation worsens. Relapse management strategies are discussed in Chapter 17.

Balanced Living

Learning to live a balanced life is an important issue in lowering your relapse risk. Chapter 18 focuses on strategies for balanced living. The better you can satisfy your needs, the less likely you are to want alcohol or other drugs.

Warning Signs of Relapse

Before you lapse or relapse, you are likely to experience both obvious and subtle warning signs that you are headed back toward substance use (Figure 16.1). These warning signs may show up in your attitudes and thoughts as well as in your behaviors and decisions.

As stated earlier, you may make decisions that initially seem to have little to do with a lapse or relapse but which, upon closer examination, are seen to be closely connected with it. For example, after being alcohol-free for 5 months, Andrew began to golf again with his former drinking buddies. By the third weekend of golf with these friends, his thoughts about having "a

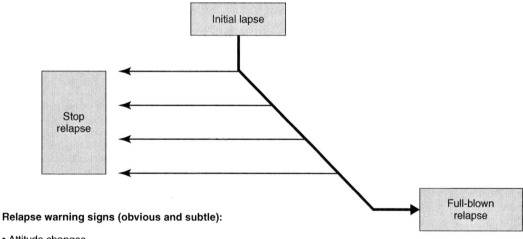

Relapse warning signs (obvious and subtle):

• Attitude changes

• Thought changes

• Mood changes

• Behavior changes

Figure 16.1 The relapse process.

few drinks" had increased significantly, and Andrew told himself, "I can't fit in unless I drink with the guys." So, he drank again. Andrew also failed to disclose during his therapy sessions that he initially thought about it, then later golfed with his old drinking buddies.

Complete the Relapse Warning Signs Worksheet to help you identify relapse warning signs and strategies for coping with them. Keep in mind that the time between the emergence of relapse warning signs and actual substance use varies greatly from person to person. The earlier you see the warning signs, the easier it will be to stop yourself before you pick up the first drink, cigarette, or other drug. Even if you have never relapsed, you will learn about relapse warning signs by the time you complete this chapter.

High-Risk Situations

High-risk situations are those in which your vulnerability to using substances is moderate to high. High-risk situations are more likely to lead to relapse if you deny or minimize their existence or don't develop effective coping strategies when confronted with them. Leading an imbalanced lifestyle is likely to put you in high-risk situations. You might feel you need to use substances to cope with upset feelings or a particular problem.

In a study conducted by one of the authors, alcoholics, smokers, and heroin addicts identified specific high-risk situations. These situations and the percentages of substance users who identified them are shown in Table 16.1.

Complete the High-Risk Situations Worksheet. This will help you identify your potential relapse risks and develop positive coping strategies. It is im-

Table 16.1 Percentages of Substance Users Identifying Specific High-Risk Situations

Relapse situation	Alcoholics	Smokers	Heroin addicts
Negative emotions	38%	37%	19%
Social pressures	18%	32%	36%
Interpersonal conflict	18%	15%	14%
Positive emotions	3%	9%	15%
Urges, temptations	11%	5%	5%
Other	12%	2%	11%

portant to think and plan ahead so that you are prepared to handle high-risk situations and will not be taken by surprise.

Homework

✎ Complete the Relapse Warning Signs Worksheet.

✎ Complete the High-Risk Situations Worksheet.

Relapse Warning Signs Worksheet

Instructions: In the left column, list the attitudes, thoughts, and behaviors that are warning signs of potential relapse. In the right column, write strategies for coping with each of these situations.

Relapse warning signs	Coping strategies

High-Risk Situations Worksheet

Instructions: List three of your high-risk situations below. For each high-risk situation, list positive coping strategies.

High-risk situation 1	Coping strategies

High-risk situation 2	Coping strategies

High-risk situation 3	Coping strategies

Chapter 17 Relapse Management:
What to Do If You Lapse or Relapse

Goals

▦ To determine and evaluate the reasons for your lapse or relapse

▦ To analyze the warning signs

▦ To learn the steps you should take when facing a lapse crisis

Learning From Your Past Mistakes

If you have a lapse or relapse, use it as a learning experience to help strengthen your recovery. Try to figure out your warning signs and the factors that led to your lapse or relapse. Use it as a motivator to change and to do things differently in your recovery.

If you have had a lapse or relapse, complete the Lapse and Relapse Worksheet to help you evaluate what led to your first drink, cigarette, or use of another drug after having quit. If you have had more than one lapse or relapse, you can complete the worksheet based on several previous experiences. Then you can determine if there are any patterns to your return to substance use.

You should always inform your therapist or counselor if you have a lapse or relapse so that you can work together to figure out what caused it and how you can get back on track. Such open discussions with your therapist will help you in the long run, even if you feel guilty or shameful about your lapse or relapse. Your therapist is there to help you, not to judge you for any mistakes that you make.

Following are examples of two individuals who discovered patterns to their return to substance use. Jason's case deals with cigarette smoking. He quit three times, only to return to smoking every time. Each time Jason returned to smoking, he had been smoke-free for at least 4 months. Marcella returned to alcohol use on four different occasions following periods of sobriety that lasted from 2 months to almost 2 years. Here's what Jason and Marcella shared about their experiences.

Case Examples

Jason (Cigarettes)

▩ *Each time I used cigarettes after a period of recovery, it was in a social situation where others were smoking and drinking alcohol. I'm not much of a drinker, but it seems real clear to me now that if I drink, I want to smoke. What I said to myself in these situations was that a few cigarettes wouldn't lead to any more use; that I'd smoke a few and quit again. This worked one time, but the other two times I bought cigarettes that night and before I knew it, I was back to smoking a pack and a half a day.* ▩

Marcella (Alcohol)

▩ *I quit drinking alcohol four different times. Once, I only had two glasses of wine with friends who took me out for dinner to celebrate my birthday. When a friend filled my wineglass I just couldn't say anything. The other three times were much worse and I drank for a couple of months during each of these relapses. When I looked at these closely, it dawned on me that when I feel bored or lonely, I somehow end up socializing with people and in situations where there's a lot of heavy drinking. It's funny because the first time or two I'm very careful not to drink in these situations even though I feel awkward. Then, it's like something comes over me when I tell myself being sober is a drag and drinking looks like so much more fun. So what to do? Simple— I drink again even though I know it's bad for me. Within a week or two I'm back to my old pattern where I drink a lot.* ▩

Identifying Your Relapse Chain

One helpful way of learning from your mistakes is to complete a Relapse Chain Worksheet. This involves a more detailed analysis in which you trace your lapse or relapse back to find warning signs that, in retrospect, you think were involved in your relapse process. Each warning sign, represented by one link in the relapse chain, involves a specific thought, feeling, or action that you believe was ultimately connected to your decision to use substances again. Complete the Relapse Chain Worksheet after reading this chapter.

Reactions to a Lapse or Relapse

The thoughts and feelings you experience following a lapse play a major role in whether or not you continue to use and move toward a full-blown relapse. Following your initial use of alcohol, tobacco, or other drugs, if you tell yourself, "I'm a failure, I can't do this, I'll never get it together" or "Since I can't stop myself from going back to using, I might as well continue," you are at high risk for a relapse because you'll be tempted to give up. If you feel excited, happy, good, euphoric, mellow, or even relieved, you may easily ask yourself, "If substances make me feel this good, why not continue to use?" On the other hand, you may feel guilty, shameful, angry at yourself, or disappointed in yourself, only to use these emotions as motivators for continued substance use. Usually, the more negative your initial reaction to a lapse, the more likely you are to say, "The hell with it" and continue using.

Similarly, your thoughts and feelings about a relapse have an impact on whether or not you take action to stop the relapse and get back on the recovery track. If you see yourself as a failure or feel guilty and shameful, you may hesitate to ask a therapist, friend, or family member for help and support.

The following case examples show how Mike, LaShawn, and Curt reacted differently to their lapses and relapses. Think about the role their thoughts and feelings played in their decisions to continue using or to stop using.

Case Examples

Mike (Cocaine)

I was out of rehab and clean for 4 months. I saw a therapist every 2 weeks and was real involved in NA. Things were going real good and I was con-

vinced I'd never use cocaine again. I ran into an old girlfriend at the mall, who invited me over to her place. I knew she was still getting high but figured I could have a good time with her and not use. Man, was I wrong. I smoked a few rocks with her and spent the night. When I got up the next day I felt real bad. I told myself I messed up and better do something before my addict side got real strong and took over. I talked to quite a few people that day and got great support. I figured out what I did wrong and decided not to see this woman again. It helped, too, to think about my daughter. Since getting clean, I've been a pretty responsible father, seeing my daughter every single week. I didn't want to mess this up. ◾

LaShawn (Pot and Opiates)

◾ *A friend stopped over whom I hadn't seen in months. After talking for awhile she asked if I wanted to get high, that she had some good herb. I told her no, I wasn't using anymore. A little later, she asked me if I minded if she lit a joint. I told her to go ahead. After watching her smoke awhile, I said to myself, "A few hits ain't really no big deal," and joined her. So I caught a buzz with her. The next day I thought to myself, "If I'm going to get high, I might as well get some good dope," 'cause pot and other drugs don't do much for me. So I picked up the phone and called my dealer. When I first shot dope again it felt so good. I mean, I really love the shit. Soon I was back into the same old pattern again where I lied, schemed, and prostituted myself to buy my dope. I didn't even bother to call my therapist or sponsor because I knew they would try to talk me out of using. About a month into my relapse, I almost called my therapist, then decided not to because I felt like I let her down. I felt I didn't deserve her help after what I did.* ◾

Curt (Cigarettes)

◾ *One year smoke-free. I couldn't believe it. I felt good and proud of what I accomplished. I'm a salesman on the road a lot. I had lunch with a customer who said he was a "chipper" and was able to enjoy a cigarette every now and then. This was a man who had a two-pack-a-day habit. It got me to thinking whether I could use his system to control my smoking. It worked! I was able to have a few now and then and really enjoy them. Of course, I had to do this in private because my wife would become very upset if she knew I was smoking again. After about a month of chipping a few days a week, I started smoking every day. Even though I was under half a pack, I could feel things gradually getting out of control. It was very disappointing for me to discover that I just can't be an occasional user. So I went back on my program and haven't smoked since.*

Reactions of Family or Significant Others

Your family or others close to you may react negatively to your return to using substances, especially if you were addicted or your substance use had caused serious problems for you or your family. Some people may be supportive and understanding, but others may become upset and angry with you. Here's what Tonie and Lindsey said about the reactions of their families. These case examples show two different responses from families.

Case Examples

Tonie (Alcohol Relapse)

My husband got very upset and frustrated when I relapsed. He basically told me that if I can't stop drinking and get back on the right track, he wasn't going to stay around. He said it bothered him to see me hurting myself and our family again and that he just couldn't take it anymore.

Lindsey (Drug Relapse)

My parents got real worried about me when I shot up again because they knew this would mess up my chance to finish college and get in medical school. Since I wasn't in any type of treatment at the time, my dad arranged for me to get detoxed and in treatment. I really didn't want to do it because I thought I should stop on my own. The truth was, I really didn't want to stop. I only went to treatment to get my parents off my back. Fortunately, something clicked along the way and it's now my choice to stay clean.

▓ *Stop, look, and listen.* Figure out what has caused you to lapse. Get out of high-risk situations immediately if there is a threat that your lapse will lead to a full-blown relapse.

▓ *Face your problems.* Deal with problems and crises immediately so that things don't build up to the point where you feel tempted to continue using alcohol or drugs.

▓ *Renew your commitment.* Remind yourself of your goals and of how important it is not to use alcohol or other drugs if you are to reach your goals.

▓ *Use your support network.* Ask family, friends, or others in recovery for help and support if needed.

▓ *Learn from your mistakes.* See what valuable lessons you can learn from your lapse. Think about ways to use this experience to help you in the future.

Homework

✎ Complete the Lapse and Relapse Worksheet.

✎ Complete the Relapse Chain Worksheet.

Lapse and Relapse Worksheet

Instructions: Answer the following questions to help you figure out what led to your first drink, cigarette, or other drug use after having quit.

1. Describe the main reason you took the first drink, cigarette, or other drug.

   _____

   _____

   _____

   _____

2. Describe your inner thoughts and feelings that triggered your need or desire for the first drink, cigarette, or other drug.

   _____

   _____

   _____

   _____

3. Describe any external circumstances that triggered your need or desire for the first drink, cigarette, or other drug.

   _____

   _____

   _____

   _____

4. Describe the first decision you made that started the lapse or relapse process.

   _____

   _____

   _____

   _____

Relapse Chain Worksheet

Instructions: The last link in the relapse chain represents your use of alcohol, tobacco, or other drugs. Each preceding link represents a specific relapse warning sign. Identify as many warning signs as you can. Then state how much time elapsed between the earliest warning sign and the first time you used a substance again. Also, state how you felt about using substances again, and how your family (or other significant people in your life) felt.

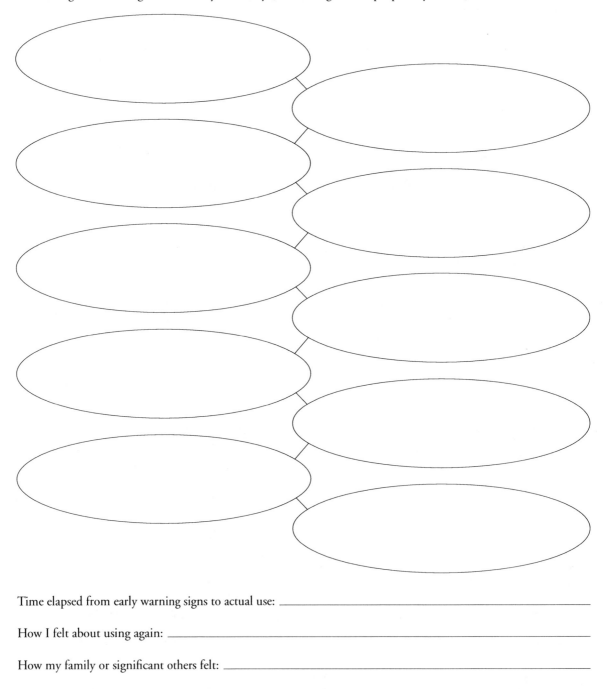

Time elapsed from early warning signs to actual use: _____

How I felt about using again: _____

How my family or significant others felt: _____

Chapter 18   *Strategies for Balanced Living*

Goals

▨ To understand the benefits of living a balanced lifestyle

▨ To determine the overall balance of your life

▨ To learn how to keep a daily inventory that will allow you to catch problems and relapse warning signs early

▨ To develop a weekly schedule of activities as a way to add structure to your life

▨ To create a list of pleasant activities

The Importance of Balance

Balance refers to the ability to reasonably manage the different aspects of your life. Balanced living is not only healthy but also serves as a protection against relapse. Balance can lead to happiness and give you an opportunity for personal growth. Although some areas of life may inevitably get temporarily out of balance, due to demands of work or family, for example, the important issue is to strive continuously for a balance that works for you and that can accommodate periods of imbalance.

Everyone has a number of responsibilities in life, or things that "should" be done. Everyone has "wants," or individual needs or interests that are important, too. Balance implies making sure that some of your "wants" get taken care of so that all your energy isn't directed toward your obligations. If your "shoulds" (obligations) greatly outnumber your "wants" (desires), your life is out of balance. One way to find this out is to list your "wants" and "shoulds" on opposite sides of the Teeter-Totter Balance Test.

One helpful way to view the concept of balance is to examine your life from each of the following major perspectives to determine any areas of serious imbalance: physical, mental or emotional, intellectual, creative or artistic, family, personal relationships, spiritual, work or school, and financial. Your particular needs in each area will depend on your personality, interests, and desire to change. Complete the Lifestyle Balance Worksheet to help you determine how balanced your life is overall. If a particular area is too much out of balance, think about steps you can take to change it. Following are examples of how others have identified areas they need to work on to achieve a greater balance in their lives.

Case Examples

Arthur (Decreasing Workaholism)

I was a workaholic. I worked 7 days a week. Even on vacations, I took work with me and called the office every day. My family relationships suffered, and I gave up playing sports, which I used to truly love. Although it was hard at first, I changed my habit of working too much by taking at least 1 day off each weekend, limiting my long days to no more than 2 each week, and planning activities with my wife and kids. I also quit using my busy work schedule as an excuse not to work out and started swimming 3 days a week. I feel better, I'm not burned out like I used to be, and my family is happier.

LeeAnn (Developing Spirituality)

My drug addiction pretty much ruined my life and caused me to lose everything important—my family, job, dignity, and too much money to count. I knew it wasn't enough for me not to use drugs, that I had to make deeper changes in myself. One thing I found helpful was to work on my spirituality. I started going back to church every week and praying. I also meditate every day for about half an hour. I'm trying to improve myself as a human being and am using my belief in God to help me. So far, things have gone pretty well. I went from feeling emotionally and spiritually bankrupt to having a sense of meaning and direction in my life. Now, I look forward to the future. I'd say that my spirituality is very important to my recovery and well-being. ■

Karen (Taking Time for Self, Using Creative Talents)

■ *I was so busy working and taking care of my family that I never took much time for myself. I've always liked writing and music, but never took much time because I put everyone else's needs first. To get a better balance, I started to do some things just for me. Now, I take some time every day, even if only a few minutes or half an hour, to read, write, or listen to music. I also joined a group of writers. We get together every 2 weeks to share our ideas and writings and to support each other. It's been great to let my creative juices flow. Plus, the new relationships I've formed have been quite satisfying because it gives me a chance to be around other people who like to write and understand the process. I feel this makes me a better mother and person now that some of my needs are getting satisfied.* ■

Daily Inventory or Review

Another practical approach to catching problems and relapse warning signs early is to take a few minutes at the end of each day to complete a daily inventory. This involves asking yourself a few questions:

■ Did any problems occur today that need my immediate attention?

■ Did anything happen today that significantly changed my desire to stay off alcohol, tobacco, or other drugs?

■ Did I experience strong cravings or persistent thoughts of using today that are still with me?

■ Did I notice any relapse indicators or warning signs today?

If you respond "Yes" to any of these questions, the next step is to develop a plan to deal with your relapse potential.

Weekly Schedule

Developing a weekly schedule of activities is one way to add structure to your life. Your schedule will also give you an overview of the different things you are spending your time on, so you have an idea of the areas that need less or more attention. A weekly schedule, if reasonably balanced, can reduce the likelihood of your feeling bored or depressed. Plus, it will help you see some of the areas you are neglecting. For example, in reviewing several of his weekly schedules, it became quite clear to Dan that his schedule was so full of work-related activities that he left little time to spend with his kids and little time for physical exercise.

You can complete the Weekly Schedule Worksheet to help plan your week. You may photocopy the worksheet from this book or download multiple copies at the Treatments That Work™ website at http://www.oup.com/us/ttw. However, although planning is especially helpful in the early phases of recovery, don't feel like you have to fill up all of your time. Leave some unstructured time so there's room for spontaneity and relaxation.

Pleasant Activities

Participating in pleasant activities is another excellent strategy for reducing boredom and depression, and for increasing positive feelings about your life. As easy as this sounds, it is difficult for many who give up using alcohol or other drugs. You can use the Pleasant Activities Worksheet to identify current pleasant activities. You can also use this worksheet to identify potential pleasant activities. This offers you the opportunity to think about new activities that you would like to try. For example, when Regina examined her list of activities, she discovered that most of her pleasant activities revolved around her husband and children. Over the years, she had gradually given up several activities she enjoyed either alone or with female friends, using the excuse that she was too busy to do these things. Unfortunately, the result was that Regina felt frustrated, resentful, and deprived. To gain more balance between her needs and the needs of her family, Regina began to take time for herself. She took a class on Chinese cooking with a girlfriend and started to go out to see new movies on occasion. Although she loves her kids dearly, Regina found the company of other adults (with no children present) to be pleasant and much needed.

Homework

✎ Complete the Teeter-Totter Balance Test.

✎ Complete the Lifestyle Balance Worksheet.

✎ Take a few minutes at the end of each day to complete a daily inventory.

✎ Complete the Weekly Schedule Worksheet to help plan your week.

✎ Complete the Pleasant Activities Worksheet.

Teeter-Totter Balance Test

Wants List	Shoulds List

Lifestyle Balance Worksheet

Instructions: Answer the following questions to help you determine how balanced your life is currently. Then review your answers. Identify two out-of-balance areas that you want to change. Write a plan for change in each area.

1. Physical:

Are you in good health?	_____ Yes	_____ No
Do you exercise regularly?	_____ Yes	_____ No
Do you follow a reasonable diet?	_____ Yes	_____ No
Do you take good care of your appearance?	_____ Yes	_____ No
Do you get sufficient rest and sleep?	_____ Yes	_____ No
Do you get regular medical and dental checkups?	_____ Yes	_____ No
Do you have strategies to handle cravings to use substances?	_____ Yes	_____ No

2. Mental/emotional:

Are you experiencing excessive stress?	_____ Yes	_____ No
Do you worry too much?	_____ Yes	_____ No
Do you have strategies to reduce mental stress?	_____ Yes	_____ No
Are you able to express your feelings to others?	_____ Yes	_____ No
Do you suffer from serious depression or anxiety?	_____ Yes	_____ No

3. Intellectual:

Are you able to satisfy your intellectual needs?	_____ Yes	_____ No
Do you have enough interests to satisfy your intellectual curiosity?	_____ Yes	_____ No

4. Creative/artistic:

Do you regularly participate in creative or artistic endeavors?	_____ Yes	_____ No
Do you have talents or abilities that you think are not being used as much as you would like?	_____ Yes	_____ No

5. Family:

Are you generally satisfied with your family relationships?	_____ Yes	_____ No
Do you spend enough time with your family (especially your children, if you have any)?	_____ Yes	_____ No
Can you rely on your family for help and support?	_____ Yes	_____ No

6. Personal relationships:

Are you generally satisfied with the quantity and quality of your personal relationships?	_____ Yes	_____ No
Do you have friends you can depend on for help and support?	_____ Yes	_____ No
Are you able to express your ideas, needs, and feelings to others?	_____ Yes	_____ No
Are there any specific relationships in which you have serious problems?	_____ Yes	_____ No

7. Spiritual:

Is there enough love in your life?	_____ Yes	_____ No
Do you pay enough attention to your "inner" spiritual life?	_____ Yes	_____ No
Do you feel a sense of inner peace?	_____ Yes	_____ No

8. Work or school

Are you usually satisfied with your work or school situation?	____ Yes	____ No
Do you spend too much time or effort working?	____ Yes	____ No
Do you spend too little time or effort working?	____ Yes	____ No

9. Financial:

Do you have sufficient income to meet your expenses?	____ Yes	____ No
Are you having any serious financial problems (e.g., too much debt, no savings, etc.)?	____ Yes	____ No
Do you handle your money responsibilities with an eye to the future?	____ Yes	____ No
Does money play too big a role in your life?	____ Yes	____ No

Out-of-balance area:

_____

My change plan:

_____

_____

_____

_____

_____

_____

Out-of-balance area:

_____

My change plan:

_____

_____

_____

_____

_____

_____

_____

Weekly Schedule Worksheet

	Sunday	Monday	Tuesday	Wednesday	Thursday	Friday	Saturday
6:00							
7:00							
8:00							
9:00							
10:00							
11:00							
12:00							
1:00							
2:00							
3:00							
4:00							
5:00							
6:00							
7:00							
8:00							
9:00							
10:00							
11:00							

Pleasant Activities Worksheet

Instructions: List current activities that you consider to be a pleasant part of your life. Then think of several new activities to try. These should be activities in which there is no or minimal pressure to use alcohol or other drugs.

Current pleasant activities

_____

_____

_____

_____

_____

_____

_____

_____

New pleasant activities

_____

_____

_____

_____

_____

_____

_____

_____

_____

Chapter 19 *Measuring Your Progress*

Goals

- To learn to define and measure the progress you've made thus far

- To recognize that progress shows in many aspects of your life, just not substance use

How to Define Progress

You can measure your progress by comparing your current status to the goals you set at the beginning of your change program. These goals may relate to your substance use; to any area of your life, such as physical, mental, or spiritual well-being or your relationships with family or friends; or to any other problem or issue that you are working on changing.

Progress is improvement or positive movement toward your identified goals. Sometimes progress is very significant and happens relatively quickly. Other times progress is less significant and happens slowly. Try to avoid the trap of judging progress in absolute or "all or none" terms, because you can be making progress even if you still have some problems. For instance, Curtis has not reached his goal of sustained abstinence from cocaine and heroin. However, in the past year he's used on fewer than 30 days, which is significantly better than his daily use during the previous year. Amanda identified the goal of "learning to cope with my anger and rage and express it appropriately." During the past 3 months, she's had only two minor episodes of lashing out at her husband and kids, a far cry better than when she lashed out a couple of times every week. Although she has gained greater control over her feelings and behavior, Amanda is still working on this problem.

Ongoing Abstinence

For many, ongoing abstinence from alcohol, drugs, or tobacco is the primary goal in the early phases of recovery. If you've been able to achieve and maintain total abstinence, that is great! Keep doing what helps you stay substance-free. If you've been unable to maintain total abstinence, try to figure out the problems that get in your way and learn from your experiences with relapse. It is not unusual for some people to make several tries at abstinence before being able to maintain it continuously.

Reduction of Substance Use

Another way of measuring progress is to see if you've reduced the amount and frequency of substance use (harm reduction). If you have been unable to achieve total abstinence but you are using smaller quantities and less often, this is a step in the right direction. You are making progress. Although total abstinence is best if you have an alcohol or drug dependency problem, reduction of use with less severe substance use problems can be a reasonable goal, but only if you don't have significant medical, psychiatric, or other problems caused or worsened by substance use. It is also best not to use any illicit drugs.

Decrease in Harmful Effects of Substances

Another way of measuring progress is to look at the effects of your substance use. If you are having fewer or less severe problems resulting from substance use, then you are headed in the right direction. For example, Melanie has managed to reduce her substance use by about 80%. She recognizes that she still needs help and is working toward total abstinence. But because Melanie has significantly reduced her alcohol use and completely stopped her marijuana use, she's had fewer disagreements with her husband, has not missed any work due to hangovers, and is not spending money that should go toward bills. Whereas she once felt like a hopeless alcoholic, Melanie now feels there is hope for her. Seeing her life improve has given her more incentive to continue working hard at achieving and maintaining total abstinence from alcohol and marijuana.

Improvement in Functioning and Quality of Life

Usually, if you stop or cut down on your substance use, you will experience improvement in the quality of your life. Jenny, for example, has more stamina when she climbs the stairs at work since she quit smoking. Denorsa is able to function as a responsible mother now that she stays off cocaine. Anthony has begun to save for his own apartment since he quit alcohol and other drugs. Jeff has gained 25 pounds and is close to his ideal body weight since quitting cocaine. The ways of measuring specific progress in the quality of your health and life are endless.

Reduction of Obsessions and Cravings

You are making progress when your desires, obsessions, or cravings for alcohol, tobacco, or other drugs are less intense, less frequent, or less bothersome. For some, it is a blessing to lose the obsession about using alcohol or other drugs. Successfully managing and living with your cravings is another indication that you are doing better.

Increase in Your Confidence in Your Ability to Cope

Feeling more confident in your ability to cope with cravings, pressures to use, or other problems is another sign of progress. Except in cases of false confidence or overconfidence, the more confidence you have in your ability to successfully cope with high-risk situations, the more likely you are to handle these situations without using.

Increased Awareness of High-Risk Situations

Another sign of progress is increased awareness of your high-risk situations and an ability to face them head-on rather than ignoring them, pretending they don't exist, or minimizing their potential to cause relapse. A greater awareness of your high-risk situations allows you to develop coping strategies. It also decreases the likelihood that you will set yourself up for relapse by putting yourself in situations in which you feel unable to resist the desire to use alcohol, tobacco, or other drugs.

Willingness to Discuss a Close Call, Lapse, or Relapse

Progress can also relate to changes in your attitude or in how you use this recovery program and work with a therapist. Even if you are still struggling with substance abuse or dependency, if you are willing to talk about lapses or relapses, close calls, and other problems you are experiencing, then you open the door for progress in your recovery. Learning to talk about yourself and to trust your therapist are good signs of progress; this helps your therapist understand and work with you.

Willingness to Change Your Recovery Plan

If your current recovery plan is not working, whether it's one you devised on your own or with the help of a therapist, then change your plan and your approach to recovery. You've no doubt heard the saying "If it ain't broke, don't fix it." The opposite is true if you aren't making progress in recovery: "If it's not working, change it."

Final Thoughts

Your willingness to become involved in a recovery program shows that you want to do something to solve your substance use problem. There are no guarantees, the work of recovery is not always easy, and progress is sometimes gradual. However, sticking with your recovery plan and changing it when it's not working can help you stop using substances and make positive changes in yourself. Keys to success include using active coping skills to manage the many challenges of recovery; setting goals and working toward them; sticking with your professional treatment until you complete it and avoiding early dropout; attending mutual support group meetings and actively participating in them; taking medications if they are prescribed; not making private decisions to quit professional treatment or mutual support group participation without discussing this with someone who knows you well; and learning from any mistakes you make.

Completing the Putting It All Together Worksheet can help you to remember and continue using the skills you've learned during your recovery. Educating yourself and learning appropriate coping skills can help you learn to manage your alcohol or drug problem and improve your life.

Homework

 ✎ Complete the Putting It All Together Worksheet.

Putting It All Together Worksheet:
What You Learned and What You Will Continue to Do to Change

1. Summarize what you learned about yourself from completing this workbook and developing a change program with your therapist or counselor.

_____

_____

_____

_____

_____

_____

_____

2. Summarize how you will continue to make positive changes in your life to help you stay alcohol- and drug-free.

_____

_____

_____

_____

_____

_____

_____

_____

Chapter 20 | *Managing a Co-occurring Psychiatric Disorder*

Goals

- ▨ To learn about the different types of psychiatric disorders

- ▨ To learn about the causes of psychiatric disorders

- ▨ To assess your psychiatric symptoms, if applicable

What Is Mental Health?

Mental "health" implies the absence of a psychiatric (mental) disorder. It involves the ability to anticipate and solve problems, manage emotions, deal with frustrations and setbacks, set goals, maintain satisfying relationships, and function responsibly in society.

A person does not have either "mental health" or a "mental disorder." Rather, there are degrees of mental health and degrees of severity of psychiatric disorders. For example, even people who are psychologically healthy can feel anxious or depressed at times. On the other hand, people with psychiatric disorders may show problems in some areas of life but do well in other areas. For example, Matt has a depressive disorder and Serena has an eating disorder. Both do well in school, yet other areas of their health and life are affected by their disorders.

Factors that protect a person or reduce the risk of developing a psychiatric disorder include (1) strong bonds with your family, community, school or church; (2) good coping skills to deal with emotions, problems, and social relationships; and (3) resiliency or ability to bounce back from difficulties.

What Is a Psychiatric Disorder?

Almost one in four adults in the United States experiences a psychiatric disorder (also called mental illness) at some point in their lives. Many people have more than one disorder. Many others also have a substance use disorder in addition to their psychiatric disorder (called "dual" or "co-occurring" disorders).

Psychiatric disorders involve a combination of symptoms that cause suffering and interfere with your ability to function. Each disorder has a set of symptoms that relate to:

- Moods (how you feel)

- Thinking (how you interpret the world or events)

- Behavior (how you act)

- Physical health (your body)

Psychiatric disorders include single-episode, recurrent-episode, and chronic or persistent types. You can experience a single episode of illness and then return to normal, or you may have several episodes over time. The length of each episode will vary, as will the amount of time between episodes. You may experience chronic or persistent symptoms over time, which require that you manage symptoms that never totally go away.

Types of Psychiatric Disorders

Mood Disorders

These involve disturbances in mood along with physical and behavioral symptoms. The most common is *major depression,* which involves feeling sad or blue, a loss of or decrease in interest in life and pleasurable activities, difficulty concentrating, appetite or sleep problems, tiredness or low energy, feelings of guilt and worthlessness, and thoughts about whether or not life is worth living. These symptoms are present most of the time, nearly every day for 2 weeks or longer.

Another form is *recurrent depression.* This involves three or more different episodes of major depression over time. Months or years may separate these episodes. About half of people with depression will have a recurrent course of this disorder.

Dysthymia is a milder but more chronic form of depression and involves feeling depressed most days for at least 2 years with two or more of the symptoms listed above in major depression. *Minor depression* involves some of the symptoms of major depression for at least 2 weeks. All forms of depression may cause personal suffering and problems in life.

Mania is the opposite of depression in that the mood is very "high" instead of depressed. Energy and activity levels increase and the need for sleep decreases. People with mania are easily distracted and their thoughts may race. During a conversation, they may jump from topic to topic. Since their judgment is affected, they may do foolish things, go on spending sprees, put themselves in danger, or get involved in a lot of activities at once.

Some people switch back and forth between depression and mania, an illness called *bipolar disorder* or *manic-depressive illness*. Some even experience symptoms of both depression and mania at the same time, a condition called *bipolar disorder, mixed type*.

Anxiety Disorders

These involve worrying too much, feeling a sense of dread, or feeling anxious or fearful. These disorders usually include both physical and mental symptoms. Many people have more than one anxiety disorder as well as depression or alcohol or drug abuse or dependence.

A *phobia* is an irrational fear of a situation or object so strong that it causes distress and problems in your life. *Social anxiety disorder* (*social phobia*) involves fear of being looked at, criticized, or rejected by others, or acting in ways that will be embarrassing or humiliating. Some people have many social situations they are afraid of, while others fear only one or two situations. Common social phobias include dating, speaking, writing or eating in public, or taking tests. *Specific phobias* involve irrational fears of situations, such as being in a closed space, being in a high place, or traveling by bus or plane, or fears of objects, such as bugs, snakes, blood, or needles. One type of phobia, called *agoraphobia*, often makes the person a prisoner at home due to the fear of leaving. Many with this disorder also have panic attacks.

Panic disorder involves sudden panic attacks in which the person feels an intense and overwhelming feeling of terror. The person may worry about going crazy or dying or feel that things "don't seem real." He or she may feel dizzy or faint, shake or tremble, sweat, feel sick to the stomach, or experience hot or cold flashes, chest pain, or a racing heart.

Obsessive-compulsive disorder involves repeating behaviors over and over like hand washing; checking doors, windows, or the stove; or counting objects many times. The person often believes bad things will happen if these rituals are not repeated a certain number of times. This disorder also involves the recurrence of obsessions or senseless and frightening thoughts, over and over again. These obsessions or intruding thoughts can relate to harming yourself or another, germs or contamination, doing something embarrassing or out of the ordinary, something "real bad" happening, your body, or sex.

Generalized anxiety disorder involves continuous, unrealistic, and excessive anxiety and worry about two or more areas of life. This anxiety and worry is accompanied by symptoms such as trembling, feeling shaky, feeling restless, shortness of breath, increased heart rate, feeling dizzy, nausea, hot flashes or chills, feeling hyper, keyed up, or on edge, trouble concentrating or "going blank," and irritability.

Post-traumatic stress disorder (PTSD) involves re-experiencing past traumatic events months or years later. They events may relate to physical or sexual assault, a natural disaster, or military combat. PTSD symptoms show up in bad dreams, intrusive thoughts, or upsetting memories and cause depression, anxiety, and severe distress.

Psychotic Disorders

Disorders such as *schizophrenia* involve unusual experiences such as hearing, feeling, seeing, or smelling things that are not there and that others do not experience. People with this illness may hear voices inside their head or have strange beliefs such as "others are out to get me" or "others are trying to put thoughts in my mind." Some exhibit strange or unusual behaviors like talking to themselves in public or dressing in a bizarre manner. Low motivation and social isolation are also common. The person may lack emotion, feel flat, feel strange, have mood swings, or feel disconnected from other people.

Eating Disorders

These include anorexia and bulimia. *Anorexia* is a disorder in which the person limits food intake and is significantly below normal body weight. *Bulimia* is a disorder in which the person eats in a binge pattern, and then induces vomiting or diarrhea to avoid gaining weight. Both disorders are associated with serious medical problems and other psychiatric disorders such as depression.

Personality Disorders

These disorders occur when longstanding personality traits, or usual ways of thinking about and dealing with life or relating to other people, cause considerable distress or difficulty. Some examples of personality traits that may cause serious problems include being impulsive and failing to plan ahead or acting before you think; avoiding situations in which you are faced with problems or conflicts with people; or being antisocial, overly controlling, passive, aggressive, self-centered, perfectionistic, or dependent.

Dual or Co-occurring Disorders

Many people have both a psychiatric and a substance use disorder. Having a psychiatric illness increases the risk of substance abuse or addiction. Likewise, substance abuse or addiction increases the risk of psychiatric illness. Alcohol and drugs can make your psychiatric symptoms worse or causes new symptoms. Some people go to a psychiatric hospital after abusing drugs like cocaine, marijuana, or alcohol and becoming depressed, manic, psychotic, violent, or suicidal.

Causes of Psychiatric Disorders

There is no simple way to explain why a given person develops a psychiatric disorder. Many biological, psychological, and environmental factors cause these disorders.

Biological Factors

Just like diabetes, hypertension, or other medical problems run in families, so do psychiatric disorders. Scientists believe that some people inherit a predisposition to develop a psychiatric disorder. There may be something in brain chemistry that puts a person at risk for developing a disorder—he or she may be "wired" differently than others. This difference—rooted in biology—shows up in personality traits and behaviors and how you process information, solve problems, and deal with your emotions. Heredity stacks the deck against some people. Therefore, it is not your fault if you have a psychiatric disorder, but it is your responsibility to do something about it and get the help you need.

Psychological Factors

How you think, your personality, and how you deal with problems or manage stress have an impact on psychiatric disorders. Some people have fewer coping skills or are more sensitive to stress, negative emotions, or inaccurate thinking than others. Others have a greater need to take risks in order to feel excitement, which can lead to problems because rules and laws are broken, and risks are taken that can have grave consequences.

Environmental Factors

Family, social, or environmental factors contribute to psychiatric illness. Examples include a chaotic home environment in which parents are not consistent with discipline, are not predictable, or are perfectionistic and too demanding. Growing up in a home with a parent who has mental illness can raise your risk of illness.

Effects of Psychiatric Disorders

The effects of a psychiatric illness depend on the type of illness, the severity of symptoms, whether or not you have more than one disorder or a coexisting substance use disorder, and your personal characteristics. Psychiatric disorders may cause or worsen problem with your physical health, relationships, ability to succeed at school or work, and self-esteem. They can cause suicidal thinking or behaviors. These disorders also create a burden for families.

Homework

 ✎ Complete the Assessing Your Psychiatric Symptoms Worksheet.

Assessing Your Psychiatric Symptoms Worksheet

Following is a brief list of symptoms of the most common psychiatric disorders. Put a check mark (√) next to the symptoms or behaviors that you currently are experiencing or you are concerned about because of past experiences.

Mood Symptoms

☐ Depression or sadness that will not go away
☐ Seldom feel pleasure or joy in life
☐ Feel hopeless or helpless
☐ Low energy or low motivation (hard to get moving)
☐ Poor appetite (eat too much or too little)
☐ Poor sleep patterns (hard to fall or stay asleep, sleep too little or too much)
☐ Hard to concentrate or solve problems
☐ Mania (high moods)
☐ Mood swings (switch back and forth between depression and high moods)
☐ Racing thoughts that are hard to control (hard to stick with one topic)
☐ Get involved in too many projects at the same time
☐ Sleep very little or go days without sleep
☐ Go on spending sprees or make bad decisions with money
☐ Get involved in risky behaviors (drug use, driving too fast, sex with strangers)
☐ Suicidal thoughts, plans or attempt

Anxiety Symptoms

☐ Severe anxiety or worry
☐ Avoiding situations that cause anxiety
☐ Panic attacks (racing heart, fears, worry about going crazy or dying)
☐ Strong fears or phobias (leaving home, flying, closed spaces, heights, animals)
☐ Bad memories, feeling or intrusive thoughts about physical/sexual abuse
☐ Obsessive thoughts (you repeat thoughts that intrude your mind)
☐ Compulsions (you repeat behaviors such as checking, counting, or washing)

Psychotic Symptoms

☐ Unusual experiences (you hear, feel, see or smell things others do not)
☐ Unusual beliefs or delusions (being special, watched by others, or paranoid)
☐ Thinking difficulty (feel confused, cannot concentrate, or have strange thoughts)
☐ Behavior changes (you stop eating or act very strange)
☐ Mood changes (you feel strange, flat or have mood swings)
☐ Negative symptoms (low motivation, social isolation, decreased thoughts)

Eating Symptoms

☐ Making myself vomit after eating
☐ Too much dieting
☐ Eating too little due to fear of gaining weight or becoming fat
☐ Constant worry about weight gain or appearance
☐ Frequent use of diuretics or enemas

Attention Deficit Symptoms

- ☐ Hard to pay attention, listen or finish things (at home, school, work)
- ☐ Hard to focus on a task for very long
- ☐ Hard to get organized (at home, work, or school)
- ☐ Feeling hyper, restless, on edge, like your "motor" is always running
- ☐ Hard to sit still for very long
- ☐ Get frustrated very easily, even with small things
- ☐ Do things impulsively by acting before thinking of consequences

Behavioral Symptoms and Relationship Problems

- ☐ Self-harm (cutting or burning self, overdosing on pills, etc.)
- ☐ Bad temper problem
- ☐ Bully, threaten or intimate other people
- ☐ Used a weapon to hurt or threaten others (bat, brick, knife, glass, gun)
- ☐ Violence towards people (hit, slap, push, punch, kick)
- ☐ Serious problems with spouse, parent or other family member
- ☐ Serious problems in relationships
- ☐ Lying, conning or deceiving others
- ☐ Trouble at work (missing days, late, getting fired, can't find or hold job)
- ☐ Trouble with school (skipping, bad grades, don't do work, kicked out/quit)
- ☐ Trouble with the law (arrested, did time in jail, on probation or parole)

Other symptoms (write in)

_____

_____

1. List below your psychiatric disorder(s). If you do not know your diagnosis, ask your doctor or therapist.

_____

2. Describe how your life has been affected by your psychiatric disorder(s).

_____

3. Describe what you hope to get out of treatment for your psychiatric disorders.

_____

_____

Appendix   *Helpful Resources*

There are many resources on alcohol and drug problems. These include informational resources (books, guides, workbooks, audiotapes, and videotapes) as well as self-help programs. In addition to the list that follows, resources can be accessed on the Internet through bookstores or publishers of recovery literature or by conducting a search of key terms or words on Google, Yahoo, or other search engine. You can search using terms such as addiction; alcohol abuse, alcohol addiction, alcohol dependence, or alcoholism; drug abuse, drug addiction, or drug dependency; families and addiction; recovery from addiction; or the name of a specific substance, person, or organization associated with research or treatment of alcohol or drug problems, addiction, or recovery.

Alcoholics Anonymous	http://www.alcoholics-anonymous.org
Al-Anon Family Groups	http://www.al-anon.org
Dennis C. Daley, Ph.D.	http://www.drdenniscdaley.com
Dual Recovery Anonymous (DRA)	http://www.dualrecovery.org
Hazelden Educational Materials	http://www.hazelden.org
Life Journal	http://www.lifejournal.com
Narcotics Anonymous	http://www.na.org
Nar-Anon Family Groups	http://www.naranon.org
National Clearinghouse for Alcohol & Drug Information	http://www.health.org
National Institute on Alcohol Abuse and Alcoholism	http://www.niaaa.nih.gov
National Institute on Drug Abuse	http://www.nida.nih.gov
National Institute of Mental Health	http://www.nimh.nih.gov

References and Suggested Readings

Information in this workbook comes from a variety of sources, including books, articles, and studies on treatment of substance use disorders, reports by the U.S. Government, books and workbooks for individuals in recovery from substance use disorders, and our extensive clinical experience over the past 30 years working with thousand of individuals with all types of alcohol and drug problems.

An asterisk (*) denotes readings for individuals in recovery.

Alcoholics Anonymous (*"Big Book"*) (4th ed). (2001). New York: AA World Services.*

American Psychiatric Association (2000). *Diagnostic and statistical manual of mental disorders* (DSM-IV-TR) (4th ed.). Washington, DC: Author.

American Society of Addiction Medicine (2002). *ASAM patient placement criteria for the treatment of substance-related disorders* (2nd ed.). Chevy Chase, MD: Author.

American Society of Addiction Medicine (2003). *Principles of addiction medicine* (3rd ed.). Chevy Chase, MD: Author.

Carroll, K.M. (1996). Relapse prevention as a psychosocial treatment: A review of controlled clinical trials. *Experimental and Clinical Psychopharmacology*, 4(1), 46–54.

Center for Substance Abuse Treatment (1999, December). *Treatment succeeds in fighting crime*. Rockville, MD: Author.

Center for Substance Abuse Treatment (2000, April). *Substance abuse treatment: Reduces family dysfunction, improves productivity*. Rockville, MD: Author.

Center for Substance Abuse Treatment (2000, May). *Treatment cuts medical costs*. Rockville, MD: Author.

Cloninger, C. R. (2005). Genetics of substance abuse. In M. Galanter & H. D. Kleber (Eds.), *Textbook of substance abuse treatment* (3rd ed., pp. 73–80). Washington, DC: American Psychiatric Publishing.

Daley, D. C. (2003). *Dual diagnosis workbook: Recovery strategies for substance use and mental health disorder* (3rd ed.). Independence, MO: Independence Press.*

Daley, D. C. (2004). *Relapse prevention workbook* (4th ed.). Apollo, PA: Daley Publications.*

Daley, D. C. (2004). *Surviving addiction workbook* (3rd ed.). Apollo, PA: Daley Publications.*

Daley, D. C. (2005). *Managing emotions: Recovery from mental health or substance use disorders.* Apollo, PA: Daley Publications.*

Daley, D. C. (2005). *Sobriety journal: Your plan for recovery in year 01.* Apollo, PA: Daley Publications.*

Daley, D. C., & Folit, R. (2006). *LifeJournal for Staying Sober and Preventing Relapse.* Retrieved March 21, 2006, from http://www.stayingsober.lifejournal.com*

Daley, D. C., & Marlatt, G. A. (2006). Relapse prevention. In J. H. Lowinson, P. Ruiz, R. B. Millman, & J. G. Langrod (Eds.), *Substance abuse: A comprehensive textbook* (4th ed., pp. 772–785). Philadelphia : Lippincott Williams & Wilkins.

Daley, D. C., & Miller, J. (2001). *Addiction in your family: Helping yourself and your loved ones.* Holmes Beach, FL: Learning Publications.*

Daley, D. C., & Moss, H. B. (2002). *Dual disorders: Counseling clients with chemical dependency and mental illness* (3rd ed.). Center City, MN: Hazelden.

Galanter, M., & Kleber, H. D. (Eds.). (2004). *Textbook of substance abuse treatment* (3rd ed.). Washington, DC: American Psychiatric Press.

Hester, R. K., & Miller, W. R. (Eds.). (2002). *Handbook of alcoholism treatment approaches: Effective alternatives* (3rd ed.). Boston: Allyn and Bacon.

Lin, S. W., & Anthenelli, R. M. (2006). Genetic factors in the risk for substance use disorders. In J. H. Lowinson, P. Ruiz, R. B. Millman, & J. G. Langrod (Eds.), *Substance abuse: A comprehensive textbook* (4th ed., pp. 33–47). Philadelphia: Lippincott Williams & Wilkins.

Lowinson, J. H., Ruiz, P., Millman, R. B., & Langrod, J. G. (Eds.) (2006). *Substance abuse: A comprehensive textbook* (4th ed.). Philadelphia: Lippincott Williams & Wilkins.

Marlatt, G. A., & Donovan, D. M. (Eds.) (2005). *Relapse prevention: Maintenance strategies in the treatment of addictive behaviors* (2nd ed.). New York: Guilford Press.

McLellan, A. T., Lewis, D. C., O'Brien, C. P., & Kleber, H. D. (2000). Drug dependence, a chronic medical illness: Implications for treatment, insurance, and outcomes evaluation. *JAMA, 284*(13), 1689–1695.

Monti, P. M., Kadden, R. M., Rohsenow, D. J., Cooney, N. L., & Abrams, D. B. (2002). *Treatment of alcohol dependence* (2nd ed.). New York: Guilford Press.

Narcotics Anonymous ("Basic Text") (1998). Van Nuys, CA: NA World Services.*

National Institute on Alcohol Abuse and Alcoholism (1999). Update on approaches to alcoholism treatment. *Alcohol Research and Health, 23*(2).

National Institute on Alcohol Abuse and Alcoholism (2000). *Alcohol and health: 10th special report to Congress.* Rockville, MD: U.S. Department of Health & Human Services.

National Institute on Drug Abuse (1999). *Principles of addiction treatment: A research-based guide* (NIH Publication No. 99-4180). Rockville, MD: Author.

National Institute on Drug Abuse (2000). *Approaches to drug abuse treatment* (NIH Publication No. 00-4151). Rockville, MD: Author.

Nowinski, J., & Baker, S. (1998). *The twelve-step facilitation handbook: A systematic approach to early recovery from alcoholism and addiction.* San Francisco: Jossey-Bass Publishers.

O'Farrell, T. J., & Fals-Stewart, W. (1999). Treatment models and methods: Family models. In B. S. McCrady & E. E. Epstein (Eds.), *Addictions: A comprehensive guidebook* (pp. 287–305). New York: Oxford University Press.

Pani, P. P., Maremmani, I., Pirastu, R., Tagliamonte, A., & Luigi Gessa, G. (2000). Buprenorphine: A controlled clinical trial in the treatment of opioid dependence. *Drug and Alcohol Dependence, 60,* 39–50.

Prochaska, J. O., Norcross, J. C., & DiClemente, C. C. (1994). *Changing for good.* New York: William Morrow.

Project MATCH (1998). Matching alcoholism treatments to client heterogeneity: Project MATCH three-year drinking outcomes. *Alcoholism: Clinical and Experimental Research, 22*(6), 1300–1311.

Robins, L. N., & Regier, D. A. (Eds.) (1991). *Psychiatric disorders in America: The epidemiologic catchment area study.* New York: The Free Press.

Schuckit, M. A. (2000). *Drug and alcohol abuse: A clinical guide to diagnosis and treatment* (5th ed.). New York: Plenum.

Volkow, N. D., & Fowler, J. S. (2000). Addiction, a disease of compulsion and drive: Involvement of the orbitofrontal cortex. *Cerebral Cortex, 10*(3), 318–325.

About the Authors

Dennis C. Daley, Ph.D., is Chief of Addiction Medicine Services and an Associate Professor of Psychiatry at the University of Pittsburgh Medical Center, Department of Psychiatry, at Western Psychiatric Institute and Clinic (WPIC) in Pittsburgh, Pa. Dr. Daley has been involved in managing and providing inpatient, partial hospital, and outpatient treatment services for alcohol and drug problems, psychiatric disorders, and co-occurring or dual disorders (substance abuse combined with psychiatric illness) for nearly three decades. He currently oversees a large continuum of over 20 treatment and prevention programs in eight community locations, serving over 8,000 consumers each year. He and colleagues were one of the first groups in the United States to develop treatment programs for substance use and co-occurring psychiatric disorders.

Dr. Daley has developed several models of treatment for substance use disorders and dual disorders described in treatment manuals. These include *Dual Disorders Recovery Counseling, Group Drug Counseling, Addiction Recovery,* and *Relapse Prevention.* He has also developed family programs and educational materials on addiction and dual disorders for families.

Dr. Daley is currently Principal Investigator of the Appalachian Tri-State Node of the National Institute on Drug Abuse's Clinical Trials Network project. He has been or is currently an investigator on 10 other NIDA- or NIAAA-funded clinical trials of treatment of addiction or co-occurring disorders. Dr. Daley is a consultant and trainer on two federally funded research projects at McLean Hospital of Harvard Medical School.

He is Co-director of the Education Core of the VISN 4 Mental Illness Research, Education and Clinical Care (MIRECC) project, a joint venture between the Pittsburgh and Philadelphia VA Health Care Systems. Dr. Daley is active in teaching and has presented over 400 workshops, lectures, and training seminars in the United States, Canada, and Europe. As a faculty member in the Department of Psychiatry, Dr. Daley provides clinical supervision to residents and provides educational lectures. He also is an Associate Professor at the University of Pittsburgh School of Social Work and previously was a faculty member in the Department of Sociology at Indiana University of Pennsylvania and the Department of Individual and Family Studies of the Pennsylvania State University. Dr. Daley has consulted with numerous social service organizations and has conducted program evaluations throughout the United States and Europe.

Dr. Daley has over 250 publications, including clinician treatment manuals, family and client educational books, workbooks, and videotapes on recovery from alcohol and drug problems, recovery from psychiatric disorders, recovery from dual disorders, and relapse prevention. He was the first professional in the United States to publish interactive workbooks on co-occurring disorders, and one of the first to publish similar materials on recovery from addiction. Dr. Daley's treatment models and recovery materials are used in numerous substance abuse and dual diagnosis treatment programs throughout the United States and other countries.

G. Alan Marlatt, Ph.D., is the Director of the Addictive Behaviors Research Center and Professor of Psychology at the University of Washington. He is renowned for his innovative theoretical and clinical work in the addictions field. Over the past two decades, he has made significant advances in developing programs for both relapse prevention and harm reduction for a range of addictive behaviors.

Dr. Marlatt is has made hundreds of presentations at scientific conferences and clinical conferences throughout the world. He has also provided many clinical workshops and consultations to substance abuse treatment agencies.

Dr. Marlatt has published numerous papers, book chapters, books, and client recovery manuals. In addition to co-editing the first editions of *Relapse Prevention: Maintenance Strategies in the Treatment of Addictive Behaviors* (1985) and *Assessment of Addictive Behaviors* (1988), Dr. Marlatt is the editor of *Harm Reduction: Pragmatic Strategies for Managing High-Risk Behaviors* (1998), co-editor of *Changing Addictive Behavior: Bridging Clinical and Public Health Strategies* (1999), and co-author of *Brief Alcohol Screening and Intervention for College Students (BASICS): A Harm Reduction Approach* (1999). His book *Relapse Prevention* is one of the most extensively cited references in the field of addiction treatment.

Dr. Marlatt is a Fellow of both the American Psychological Association and the American Psychological Society and is a former president of the Association for Advancement of Behavior Therapy. He served as a member of the National Advisory Council on Drug Abuse at the National Institute on Drug Abuse from 1996 to 2002 and served on the National Advisory Council on Alcohol Abuse and Alcoholism Subcommittee on College Drinking from 1998 to 2001. Dr. Marlatt currently holds a Senior Research Scientist Award from the National Institute on Alcohol Abuse and Alcoholism and received the Innovators Combating Substance Abuse Award from the Robert Wood Johnson Foundation in 2001. Previously he was presented with the Jellinek Memorial Award for Alcohol Studies (1990), the Distinguished Scientist Award from the American Psychological Association's Society of Clinical Psychology (2000), the Visionary Award by the Network of Colleges and Universities Committed to the Elimination of Drug and Alcohol Abuse (2002), and the Distinguished Researcher Award from the Research Society on Alcoholism (2004).